My Ordinary Son

by
Debra J. Zabierek

Bloomington, IN Milton Keynes, UK

authorHOUSE®

AuthorHouse™
1663 Liberty Drive, Suite 200
Bloomington, IN 47403
www.authorhouse.com
Phone: 1-800-839-8640

AuthorHouse™ UK Ltd.
500 Avebury Boulevard
Central Milton Keynes, MK9 2BE
www.authorhouse.co.uk
Phone: 08001974150

First published by AuthorHouse 9/11/2006

ISBN: 1-4259-5366-2 (sc)

Library of Congress Control Number: 2006907427

Printed in the United States of America
Bloomington, Indiana

This book is printed on acid-free paper.

<u>This book is dedicated to:</u>

My beautiful daughters Ashley and Alyssa, you both are the lights that guide my path. Continue the legacy of "My Ordinary Son".

I would like to thank my family and friends for always being there for me. I especially thank my parents and my in-laws for beginning the foundation on which Gary and I built our family. I also thank my dearest friends Kathy, Paul, Judy and Art. To my "Constant Gardener" Donna I would not have grown without your support and daily telephone calls. I would also like to thank Dr. Jennifer A. Smith, Director of Assessment and Instructional Personnel for the Methuen School Department. Your time and advice meant a great deal to me.

Last but certainly not least, I thank my dear, devoted, husband Gary. I would not have had the courage to write this book without your faith in me. Your endless love and support has sustained me. Having you by my side allowed me to raise an "Extraordinary Son".

My love to you all,
Debra

<u>Turning Point</u>

"Look to the right of you and look to the left of you. One of the three of you will end up having a cesarean section delivery," said the birthing class instructor. I thought to myself immediately that it definitely would not be me. I was going to have a very ordinary delivery like every other mother I knew. Several weeks later not only did I have a cesarean delivery, but it was an emergency delivery. Due to medical complications, I was separated from my baby. I delivered an eight pound nine ounce baby boy; however, I could not see him or hold him. I was devastated. I had planned a better ending to my pregnancy. Isolated in a private room, fear began to seep into my bones. I started to believe that I had lost my baby and everyone was afraid to tell me. Fortunately medication brought on sleep and the night passed. I awoke the next morning to a visit from the pediatrician. He informed me that my baby was healthy and he had just instructed the nurse to bring him to me.

I sat up in my bed and eagerly waited. I began to hear the turning wheels and wondered if it was the sound made by a moving bassinet. The sound slowed as it approached my room. Could this be him? Suddenly, a nurse appeared with a bassinet! She stopped right next to my bed. I watched with hungry eyes as she reached into the bassinet and picked up a tiny bundle wrapped in blue. She placed him gently into my eagerly awaiting arms.

Overwhelming love consumed me. The bond to him was instant, and all doubts and fears were washed away. As I kissed him and counted fingers and toes, I planned a wonderfully ordinary life, raising my son. My son died 19 years, 8 months, and 9 days later. It was only then that I realized that I had given birth to and raised a very extraordinary son.

This story is my journey through the grief and recovery from losing a child. All parents imagine that they could not go on or handle the death of their child. I had the very same thoughts every time I heard of a tragedy involving a child. "How could I go on?" I would ask myself. I thought that I would have to be committed to an institution, for surely I would go insane if I faced such a horror. I did face such a horror on June 30, 2002, when my son, Aaron Keith Zabierek, was killed in a car accident. I would like to share my experience in the hopes of enlightening you to what a parent goes through when a child dies.

It was a bright, sunny Sunday in June. The weather could not have been more perfect. My daughter Alyssa, fourteen years old, and I had just returned from a dance competition. Alyssa has been dancing since she was five years old. My husband of twenty- one years, Gary, and my seventeen-year- old daughter Ashley were sitting by the pool enjoying the day. Aaron was at work; he was a waiter. Alyssa asked to have some of the dancers over to swim in the pool and to celebrate the end of the dance competition. We were all sitting by the pool enjoying a back yard barbecue. Aaron returned home at 5:00 P.M. I can still see him walking into the back yard as if it were yesterday. He was incredibly tall at six feet four inches. He looked so handsome to me. I thought this and to this day regret that I did not tell him. He was happy because he had officially begun his vacation. The restaurant was closed for one week. I remember asking Aaron if he realized what the next day was. He replied, "It's the old buck's birthday." Gary's birthday was the next day. He stood behind Gary and squeezed his father's shoulders in affection.

Aaron enjoyed a hamburger with a glass of my homemade iced tea. He thought I made the best iced tea in the world. Grandpa asked Aaron to help install the gate on the back yard fence. My in-laws live with us in an in-law apartment. Aaron helped Grandpa. He would always help any time he was asked. He may have grumbled, but he would never answer with a no. He then decided to wash his new car. He had just bought the 1998 Ford Taurus five weeks earlier. My husband and I co-signed his loan reluctantly. It was a big responsibility for him. He was so excited about the car and promised to make the payments and treat the car like gold. He was true to his word, for he washed that car every week. Nana asked him to wash her car too. He did that for her as well. While we lingered by the pool, he tried to squirt us with the hose. The girls screamed wildly from the water. I can still see his big blue eyes peeking over the fence as he tried to reach me with the hose. Fortunately he never did! Gary and I cleaned up the remainder of the barbecue. As I walked by Aaron, he was leaning over his hood wiping it with a cloth. I asked him, "Do you have any money for me?" He had been giving me his paycheck to cover the loan payment on the car. Aaron and I were working together to help get his finances on track. He said,"Yes, I'll give it to you when I am done washing my car."

He came into the house about 6:30 p.m. Ashley and Gary were getting ready to go rent a video. Ashley was being punished and had to stay in the house that night. I had Alyssa tell the girls that they had to go home by 8:00 p.m. I was tired and wanted to enjoy the movie quietly. Aaron came downstairs and gave Gary his pay. I told him to keep $30.00 for spending money. He also had three one-dollar bills in the pay. My husband told him, "Take the ones. I don't want your lousy three dollars!" Aaron put the $33.00 in his pocket. At 7:00 p.m. he came back downstairs. He stood at the edge of the room and peeked around the corner and said, "Mom, I am going for a ride to dry off my car. I'll be back in a while."

Gary, Ashley, and I were watching the video. At about 7:30 p.m. a trauma truck drove down the street. We live near a lake, and I commented that someone might have drowned. My husband disagreed with me and stated that someone must have had a heart attack. He believed they would not send a trauma truck for a drowning. How ironic that we discussed the details of a life in trouble. Does it matter why the truck was needed? (After all, the truck was for our son and we did not even know). At 8:00 p.m. I stated that he had been gone a long time for a quick ride. My husband gave me the typical father look. I knew he was thinking that Aaron had decided to stop at a store or a friend's house. He was nineteen years old. I let it go. Aaron was very good about calling if he was going to be delayed. Alyssa's friends were picked up, and all were gone by 8:15 p.m.

At 9:00p.m. sharp two police cars pulled into our driveway. I immediately thought that Aaron was in trouble. He had done something wrong, and I was instantly nervous and angry. The police approached my door, but a woman was with them. I thought he must have hit her car and took off. Why would a woman be with the police? I began to shake. The police officers introduced themselves. They introduced the woman as a representative from the trauma intervention unit. I screamed immediately that my son was dead. The officer spoke those words made famous on television: "His injuries were too severe. He did not survive the accident." I still hear the screams echoing in my head. My youngest daughter was in her bedroom. She had to hear this screaming and was informed of her brother's death from a stranger. I was unable to comfort my children. That is one of my regrets. My daughters needed me, but my own grief disabled me from comforting them that night.

My first thought was the location of the accident. He must have been on the highway near the city? I asked the officer, "Where was he?" I was not prepared for the answer I received; "He was down the street, ma'am, on Poplar Hill Road." He was minutes from our house. How could this happen? Why did this happen? The only other memory of the officer's conversation I have is that he told me it was a single vehicle accident and no one was in the car with him.

This is a time when family and friends play the most important role in your life. It is amazing how instantly you are unable to function. To even be incapable of sipping a glass of water. My house filled with family and friends. They gathered details from the police officers, obtained medication for us and comforted my daughters. A fog surrounded us. You feel like you are in a dream state, watching people move around you. I was a robot moving at the commands of my loved ones. People came to comfort us. There were so many. I do not remember all of them. The priest was also summoned. He did little to comfort me. I remember asking what would happen to Aaron because he did not receive last rites. He replied, "God remembers the good." This did not help ease my worries. Aaron was friends with another priest at my parish. I asked for him. A friend agreed to track him down. I knew he would be able to comfort me.

Midnight soon arrived and the volume of people in the house dwindled. My youngest daughter reached out to me. She could not sleep. The mother instinct finally surfaced, and I lay down in an attempt to comfort her. She fell asleep. My love for her came through but was then quickly clouded. I'd never be the mom I was. I wandered downstairs to find my husband sitting alone. We still had not connected in grief. He was the only person in the world who could understand what I felt. However, our grief separated us instantly. We sat and stared blankly. There was a knock at the front door. A co-worker and close friend of Aaron's was at the door. I will never forget the look on his face. He could not come in to visit with us; he only wanted to say that he had to come to tell us, "He was the best kid I ever knew." I could see his raw pain and grief. I believed at that moment that I was no longer alone in my pain. The friend left and my husband and I went to bed. It seemed to be the next step. We lay in bed holding each other. We had finally connected in grief. The night took an eternity to pass. Each of us was awake but unaware of the other. We did not want to steal the peace we thought the other must have while sleeping. No sleep occurred in my bedroom that night. I only prayed over and over again to God. I begged him to make it a dream. I believed he had the power to change the events of June 30, 2002. I would have sold my soul to erase that night.

The Day After

Ironically, the day after my son died was my husband's birthday. His birthday is now tainted, for it will be remembered as the first day of our lives without Aaron. At 5:00 a.m. neither one of us could take lying in the bed any longer. I remember going downstairs and then thinking, what now? What do we do? Should I make coffee? Even that simple daily task seemed overwhelming to me. I immediately searched for a picture of Aaron. I found one that captured his essence. There were not enough pictures of him. I have a habit of being a camera buff and actually have an incredible number of pictures. However, all pictures are taken with the thought that there will be more to follow. Who would ever take a photo with the thought that it is the last picture to be taken of that person? No picture seemed right.

My feelings of guilt and regret were immediate. Every negative moment or thought is what surfaced. Every action I had taken was regretted because I could have done better. My deepest ache came from the fact that I did not physically touch my son the day he died. He was nineteen and past the 'kiss goodbye' phase. We did not have to identify his body as they do in the movies. I was obsessed with remembering the last physical contact. Did I love him enough? My husband did not understand this. So many times I have been told, "Aaron knew you loved him." I would ask, "Did he really?" Did I love him enough? Can't I have one more hour with him? Why couldn't he be in a coma? I could touch him and tell him that I loved him with every ounce of my being.

My parents and in-laws must have had the same night as us, for they came to the house at 6:30 a.m. I am sure hundreds of people shared that long, draining night. My dad had spoken with the police and also contacted the funeral parlor. That is what is done almost immediately. I remember him telling me that Aaron's body had to be autopsied. I knew it must have been to check for drugs and alcohol. I wanted to scream that they could not touch my son. I'm a CSI fan, and I thought of Aaron being on that cold, steel table. Fortunately, very early the call came that the accident was just that, an accident. An autopsy would not have to be done. I thanked the Lord for one small favor.

As family, friends, kids, and priests came, I remember seeing the pain in their eyes. I would actually feel sorry for them while they tried to comfort me. No words could help. Nothing could be said. The presence and touches from them were my medicine. That is what I needed. There is some comfort in being surrounded with people. It's like a blanket that you can sink into and escape the outside world.

There was a knock on my door at 7:00 a.m. It was a reporter from the local newspaper. That was the first anger I felt. I screamed, "My son is not even dead a day and you want a story!" Gary and my dad stepped outside to talk to him. He was honest and said that he had to do the story. He could write his version, or Gary could give him the truth. God bless my husband for speaking to the man. The first comment my husband gave was that Aaron was a former Methuen High Band member. The reporter was also a former band geek. A connection was made. I thank that reporter today. He wrote a beautiful, memorable story about my son. We say to Aaron now, "Hey, you made the front page and you even got a color picture!" We were spared the usual photo of the car and scene. Looking back, I am grateful for that.

My son had become close to a priest while he was enrolled in the confirmation program at the local Catholic Church. He and a friend's daughter visited often with Father David. Father David was responsible for bringing the faith back into our lives as well as Aaron's. My friend contacted Father David, and he came directly to our home that morning. I've often heard that it is common for people to lose their faith at a time like that. I may have done that if it weren't for Father David. His words of comfort were more real because he knew Aaron so personally. I could see the love and pain in his eyes. I expressed my concern because Aaron had not received last rites. I was afraid that Aaron was alone. The family members that died before Aaron were older, and I was afraid he would not remember them. Father David's assurance that Aaron was with Jesus comforted me. He reminded me that Aaron was a kind, loving person. The life he lived represented the kind of soul who entered heaven. Father David also told us a wonderful story about Aaron. Father David, Aaron and some friends had climbed Mount Monadnock a couple of years ago. They began their ascent on the mountain. Aaron was not in good shape at the time. He struggled while they climbed the mountain. Everyone struggled because Aaron did. He joked about Aaron needing frequent rests and a bathroom! We all shared a moment of laughter. When they finally made it to the top of the mountain, Aaron looked out over the mountain and said, "Look at God's creation and how beautiful it is." This enabled Father David to lead the group in a spiritual discussion. He told us, "Aaron had a way of letting you see the world through his eyes. You saw the good times and you saw Aaron's pain! I ask Aaron now to please let me see heaven through his eyes." This spiritual connection to Aaron was healing for me. The story also changed the way I had been seeing my son. I connected to his life and thought a good thought for the first time since I had heard the fateful news. He also blessed Aaron's body when it arrived at the funeral parlor. I believed that this was the next best thing to having last rites. He erased my concerns.

The trip to the funeral parlor came next. My parents took the responsibility of taking my husband and me. Father David also came with us. He is truly a kind and compassionate priest. My previous contact with a funeral parlor had only been to attend a wake or funeral. I had never been behind the scenes. Once again people lead you through the steps and decisions. Shortly after we were seated in the family area, the director told us that they had just brought in Aaron's body. I was not prepared for that. How could my child be in the next room and I could not touch or see him! (It was at this point that Father David left the room to bless Aaron. Father David is the only friend or family member that saw my son dead). I was instantly terrified of the future. I wanted to run until I could no longer run. The pain is so unbearable; inside you go away to a dark place. You can almost see yourself as a separate person from your soul. You move through a fog. I might have asked how he died. I don't know. The director handed us the coroner's report. We read it. It simply stated that death was immediate and the cause was multiple, blunt impact injuries. He did tell us that Aaron looked all right, so there could be an open casket. I was relieved. I could touch my boy and see him when I said goodbye. I still feel guilt because I did not ask to see his body. Part of me is glad I did not have to see him in that way. My memory of him is whole, standing in my living room with a peaceful look on his face.

We selected thank you cards and other items. I don't remember many details. However, I do remember selecting the casket. They are set up in a separate room. There are many colors and styles to choose from. It is almost like shopping for furniture. My husband and I both snapped back to reality at this point. We were very specific about selecting one for Aaron. It was going to be his next home, and we are both particular about choosing things for our children. I am glad that we could get through that step. I could not describe it in detail today, but I remember seeing him in it and thinking we chose the right one.

We arrived home to the remainder of my immediate family waiting for us in the driveway. One of my three brothers and one of my two sisters were away and could not return the night Aaron died. I think now how awful it must have been for them. The urgency to come to my house and not being able to. It is truly odd how, at times, you feel sympathy for the ones around you. Seeing them brought me back to the night before. This moment was rock bottom for me. Having all of my family present and going to the funeral parlor made it no longer a dream. I felt for my husband. His one sibling was in California and would not arrive until the next day. It was sad for him to not have his whole family with him. I even remember feeling how awful for his sister to sit alone on a plane after hearing such tragic news. My sister ran to me and hugged me. She assisted me into my house. I can still feel her hands on my face comforting me. At that moment I felt like the child. I just wanted someone to take care of me.

I slept for a while on my couch. There was much activity around me. Deliveries of flowers and food began to arrive immediately. A close friend came by. I missed her because I was out cold while she was at my house. Again the guilt of not speaking to her surfaced. I was always a hostess. My husband and I entertained quite often. I was used to having people in my house. I should be waiting on them, not the other way around. Every thought and action is clouded with confusion. How do I act? Our society never discusses these events. I have limited memory of that day. I can't even place my daughters at home that day. I've always thought of myself as a good mother. I attended every school event and was there for my children. I don't even know if my daughters actually needed me. I do remember friends coming by for them. I thought how good of them to be there for the girls. I think I was comforted in the fact that they had their own to take care of them. So many people came by. I wondered if I would have the courage to visit a friend in such times of horror. I am blessed that people had the courage to see us. They all would tell me that they knew I would do it for them so they had to do it for me. Would I?

The questions began on that second day. I wanted to know how the accident happened. I wanted to know who found him. I also wanted to know what the car looked like. The most pressing question I had was what time he actually died. I could not understand how he could have been lying in the road, just minutes from my house, and I felt nothing. Why didn't I sense this? Shouldn't a mother feel her son taking his last breath? If I sensed it, I would have run to him. I could have said goodbye. I could have touched him. My questions, except one, had no answers. We were told that Aaron was not speeding and he must have avoided something in the road. He hit the only telephone pole in that section of the road. I thought of him sitting in his car with his head resting against the steering wheel. That was a picture I could not erase from my head.

I did have one other question that my husband did not. I wondered if Aaron had taken his own life. I thought that maybe I had been too hard on him about his finances. Maybe he had problems that we were unaware of. I did not hold on to this question very long before I got an answer. A close friend of Aaron, the one who came at midnight the night before, came by again that night. Everyone had gone home when he came. He visited with my husband and me. This friend had spent the most time with Aaron during the past year. Aaron would go to his house to hang out every night after work. All of Aaron's other friends were still away at college, so he bonded with this friend from work. I asked him directly if he thought that Aaron would have done this on purpose. He answered me firmly, "No." He told us that Aaron was on top of the world. He was excited to have his new car. He planned to clear up his financial situation. They even talked of joining the Marine Reserves. He believed it was an accident. He, with friends, had looked at the road closely to re-create the events. He believed Aaron must have avoided a deer in the road. He said it was common to see deer in that stretch of road. He asked us to see the car. He wanted to look at it closely in hope of finding an answer for the accident. We had to tell him no. That morning a close friend and my brother went to the garage where the car had been towed. After they did the horrific task of cleaning out the car, it was taken away. We told Aaron's friend that we accepted it as an accident and did not want further investigating. It would not bring Aaron back. The crash was ruled as an accident. My husband also feared that we might end up seeing the car. He did not want to look at the car, and he wanted to keep me from seeing it as well.

This friend also described his friendship with Aaron. He told us that Aaron was the best kid he ever knew. He said that his parents actually knew Aaron. He was the first friend that his parents took the time to get to know. He said that Aaron would have never steered him down the wrong path. He said, "Aaron was the kind of guy who would never end up missing his front teeth, lying on the side of the road, in a gutter, weighing only eighty pounds." His rough comment warmed my heart. Aaron had touched his life with such positive actions to make this boy have these feelings. You hold on to the good at these times. It's as if the good gives you the energy to take another breath. I believe God sent that boy to me that night and I am thankful.

The Wait

We chose to have the funeral on Saturday. Because the Fourth of July holiday was that week, we had less time to pick a day. When do you want to bury your child? I chose never. Is that an option? No, we had to select a day. There were people flying in from out of town, so we did not want to rush and have it before the holiday. We decided to have the wake on Friday from 4:00 p.m. to 9:00 p.m. We had four days to wait. People asked me if waiting so long helped or made it worse. I don't know the answer to that because I was not in the other situation. Every day that passed that week brought me closer to seeing my son. Yet every day that passed brought me closer to saying goodbye. I could not imagine that final goodbye. Just as people say to me that they could not imagine going through such a thing, I could not imagine it either. The longer I waited, the more I believed that a mistake had happened. I would look out my front window and imagine seeing his car pull into the driveway. I pictured him walking through the front door asking, "What is all the company for? Are we having a party?" Sadly, he never walked through the front door again.

I woke the second day very early. Those first seconds opening my eyes were the only peace I felt. I forgot for a brief moment. However, the moment I rolled over to get out of bed, reality hit me as I saw his picture on my nightstand. Seeing that picture said to me that it wasn't a dream…it had really happened. That morning, I let my husband sleep. I wandered downstairs. I remember taking some towels and attempting to wash them. The confusion of deciding what to do next overwhelmed me. If I sat still, thoughts of Aaron filled my head. If I tried to do something, I did not have the energy to complete a task. Every moment I thought that I would not make it to the next. I simply wanted to quit my life. Taking a breath was even difficult. As I stood at the washing machine, these thoughts roamed my head. I wanted to quit. Suddenly I heard a noise. I went into my living room, and my brother and his wife were at my front door. He had heard me say that the moment we awoke was the hardest part of the day. That was the quiet time when we actually had to think for ourselves. He came to my house to ease those moments. He came bearing gifts of Dunkin Donuts coffee! I woke my husband. We sat and savored the company and coffee. My brother and his wife stayed with us until our parents arrived. I remember him saying, "Well, the second shift is here, and we can go now." I never did find out who finished washing those towels.

I wandered into Aaron's room and looked around. I had the desire to touch everything in his room. I opened a trunk of his and found a folder on top. There was an essay in it that he had written in college. Aaron had attended Norwich University as a cadet for one semester immediately after high school. He left NU in January of 2001. In the folder was a note from me that I had sent to him while he was away. The note was a typical mom note, filled with love and things about being proud of him. I held that note to my heart. It was if he was telling me that he knew I loved him. I did say it in the note many times. He saved the note so I had proof that he knew I loved him. I had a moment of peace. There was also a note from my sister. She wrote it the day Aaron graduated from high school. He had recently cleaned his room. I had hounded him for weeks to clean the mess. He was a messy guy. He went to a military college for a semester, and they could not change his messy habits! I read the essay. He wrote about the time his girlfriend broke up with him. He titled it The Worst Day of My Life. He wrote about such despair. That event hurt him deeply. He was in pain. As I read his words, I realized that he felt more pain than I remembered. I asked myself, why didn't he share this with me? I felt such sorrow for him. He included a quote in the essay. "What does not kill you can only make you stronger." Is this a message for me? Am I supposed to gather strength from losing my son? It was at that moment that I began to think, "What would Aaron want me to do?" If he were here, how would he advise me? I held on to that essay and my letter. They were like gold to me.

My husband and older daughter could not go into his room that week. If you went into that room, he was still alive. His scent permeated the space. That feeling was too much for them. I needed that feeling that week. I wanted to smell him and see everything that was his. I thought the room held an answer for me. I don't know what I was looking for. Maybe his things told a story about him that I did not know. At nineteen years of age, he was very independent. We saw very little of him because he was a waiter and worked from late afternoon until our bedtime. When your children are babies, you know every step they take, every breath they take, and almost every thought. The babies grow into adults and the control disappears. I know it is natural, but when you lose a child you remember the control and wish you never had to let go. I wanted to know every step, breath, and thought he took. I believed the room would give me the answers. I began my search.

A book caught my eye. It was by John Edward. There was a receipt from a video store in the book. I held that receipt and wondered if he enjoyed the movie. Did I ask him about it? Was I too busy to talk with him that week? Even things that seem useless can bring a thousand questions leading to guilt and more sorrow. I left the room because I could not bear to be in it any longer. I took the book.

My daughters did not have anything to wear to the wake or funeral. They are typical teenage girls with a vibrant wardrobe. Nothing in their closet seemed appropriate. My youngest sister and sister-in-law offered to take them shopping for outfits. Gary gave them some money, and at first they would not accept it. Gary insisted and he said, "A dad is supposed to take care of his children. Let me take care of my children." The pain in his eyes reached to his soul. We were devastated to see his pain. They accepted his money. To this day if I am struggling or having a moment, as we call it, I understand it. I know that I will come out of it. However, when I see my daughters or husband struggle, it breaks my heart. I wonder if their pain is deeper than I can see. The crazy thoughts come into my head. I worry that they may be slipping away from me. This is the hardest part of my journey. The desire for them to be okay is so intense that when they stumble I can't bear it. I lost one loved one; I could not stand to lose another.

My parents told us that we had to choose a cemetery. Our purpose that day was to visit a few and decide which was the best home for our son. I remember my husband telling me to take a shower. I did what I was told. I took my shower and was then led to the car for a tour of the cemeteries. My husband's uncle was buried in a cemetery that overlooked a stream. I wanted Aaron to be in a peaceful, quiet spot. I did not want my son to be lost in a sea of gray stones. I wanted him to stand out with a tree or hill to mark his spot. My parents drove us by some cemeteries. I could not get out of the car. We went to the funeral parlor. The director told us immediately that we could not choose the cemetery where my husband's uncle was buried because it was closed.

My heart was crushed. What would I do now? That funeral director asked me why I wanted that cemetery. I told him that I liked the trees. He thought he could help me achieve what I wanted. He took us to Elmwood Cemetery, the town cemetery. He selected a spot right under a tree on a corner. It was not my first choice, but at least I could point to a tree to find him. He would not be one gray stone in a row of one hundred. He was going to stand out just as he had in life.

There was a moment that day when the pain was the same as it was when we received the news of Aaron's death. When we arrived at the funeral parlor, we asked the director for the necklace that Aaron was wearing. He brought it out to us, but then stated that Aaron's wallet was missing. My husband asked about money in his pocket. The director left the room and came back with Aaron's shorts. To see his shorts was horrifying. They were his favorite shorts. This must be real. The shorts were dotted with Aaron's blood. I was silently horrified. I could not touch the shorts. My husband reached into a pocket and pulled out the $33. Seeing that money broke my heart. He took the money, went for a ride, and died. It was true. They did not make a mistake. How could they get the exact amount of money and Aaron's favorite khaki shorts? Such a simple task, the director handing Gary the shorts, causing deep pain and unbearable sadness.

On the ride home from the cemetery, I gathered all of my strength and asked to be driven by the crash scene. Similar to others I had seen on television, the crash site was decorated with candles, flowers, and pictures, I was told. The kids seemed to gather there. Aaron's former girlfriend intended to hold a candlelight vigil on this night. To my surprise my parents and Gary agreed to drive by. As we approached the site, one would not know a child had died on that spot if it weren't for the flowers and candles. The road looked no different to me. I expected to see trees down and the stone wall that lined the road destroyed. To the contrary, I could not pick out the spot on my own. Had the memorial not been created, I would not have picked out the fateful spot. As we passed the site, I felt nothing. I did not react at all. I could not sense Aaron being there, nor did it bring tears. I'm glad I went to see the memorial constructed for him, but it neither comforted me nor saddened me.

It is amazing to me how people come through at a time of tragedy. We were inundated with flowers, plants, fruit baskets, food baskets, money, books, letters and gifts. It seemed that every several minutes a gift arrived. People reached out to us in a way that is typical of a good neighbor. Among the items were two air conditioners. It was oppressive that week, and the heat was unbearable. My brother was concerned that we wouldn't sleep because of the heat. He delivered an air conditioner for Gary and me. When one of my daughter's friends' mothers heard about this, she also delivered one for the girls' room. I remember coming out of the bathroom and being frustrated that even though I was grieving, I still had to change the toilet paper! I used the last roll! Later that day we received one hundred rolls of toilet paper. It took us months to use up all of that toilet paper. I remember taking out the last package and saying, "This is the last roll of funeral paper." Sometimes humor is the only way to survive.

I believe it was at this point that I picked up the John Edward book and began to read it. Aaron had been very interested in John Edward. He had heard about John Edward from a family friend in the fall of 2001. I have a very dear friend that I have known since I was seven years old. She has two sisters. One sister's husband's name was Keith. He was the one that introduced Aaron to the topic of conversing with the other side. I refer to Keith in the past tense because he was killed in a car accident almost the same way as Aaron was, just five weeks before Aaron's death. He also veered off the road and was killed instantly.

The only immediate difference is that Keith had witnesses. These witnesses saw him do just as I described. An autopsy was not done. We do not know for sure why Aaron or Keith suddenly turned off the road. Ironically, both of them were driving black Fords and veered to the left of the road. Aaron and Keith were very similar in stature. They were also both similar in personalities. One would describe each as one of the good ones. Both were kind and compassionate with many friends. What are the chances that my friend and I would suffer a similar tragedy just five weeks apart? When I went to Keith's service, I was distraught. I remember thinking that it was the saddest and most difficult thing I had to do in my life. Little did I know that I would face the most difficult event in my life in just five short weeks. I do not believe their deaths were a coincidence. Aaron and Keith are strongly connected. I believe they are together on the other side. The timing of their deaths holds a message for me, and I continue on my journey to unlock the answer.

Aaron read the book and watched the program on television. He would describe the show to me in the hopes that I would watch it. I thought it was unusual for Aaron to be interested in this topic. I was always drawn to the psychic world. I had drifted from it after a reading from a medium years ago. She talked about my children and that bothered me. Gary and I bought Aaron one of John Edward's books for Christmas. Prior to the initial visit to the funeral parlor, the director requested photos of Aaron for reference. Someone looked through our albums and pulled out a couple of pictures of Aaron. One picture had been taken of Aaron Christmas morning, and he was holding the John Edward book. Was that a coincidence? I considered this as my first sign. I regret now that I never discussed this topic with Aaron in depth. John discussed the afterlife in detail. One area that captured my attention was that loved ones send signs from heaven to let those left behind know they go on and are okay. I immediately began asking Aaron for signs. I asked Aaron to send me a trumpet sign.

Aaron was a trumpet player. He had begun playing the trumpet in fourth grade and continued through high school. He was in the Methuen marching band, concert band, and jazz band. Ironically, he played Taps at funerals. He also played Taps for the Methuen Fire Fighters Memorial Service. Aaron continued with his music at Norwich University. He was the regimental bugler. Aaron was also a key player in organizing a small band for the local church, during his confirmation training. The kids would play at the Sunday 5:00 P.M. mass. There was a drummer, flutist, saxophone player, and a keyboard player. Aaron's girlfriend was the flutist. She was not Catholic but joined the kids. When Aaron was out in town, people would stop him and say to him, "You are the trumpet player in church. It is so nice to hear the trumpet in church." Aaron was a tall, handsome, blonde-haired, blue-eyed guy. I would look at him with such pride and love. I hope he glanced at me to see that look. It was during this time in church that Aaron and the kids got to know Father David personally. Aaron and one of his friends, the daughter of our best friends, became Eucharistic Ministers after they were confirmed. Father David opened the door to faith for them and, in doing that, the door was opened for me as well.

I continued to read the book. I wanted to connect with Aaron. By reading the book, I could learn something about my son. I wondered if something led me to the book in his room. I am a Catholic. I believe in Jesus and God. I also believe in ghosts. This background gave me the courage to explore the afterlife.

His Life in Pictures

The funeral parlor director had given us a board to display pictures of Aaron. Family and friends offered to create a collage of Aaron's pictures for me. I insisted on doing this myself. My mother helped me. I don't know how she did it, and I thank her today. I was determined to finish it and was a bit crazy. My husband and daughters could not help with this task. My mother, mother-in-law, sister, aunt, and others helped me in the beginning. I gathered all of my photo albums. We placed the board on the dining room table and proceeded to make the collage. I was so driven that I scared everyone away except my mother. We continued with the project. I wanted to capture every part of Aaron's life. I wanted this board to tell a story about him. I chose a picture of Gary and me going to a Lamaze class and put this in the center. I then selected pictures of him by age to radiate out from the center. We must have looked at a thousand pictures. My friends and family were incredibly supportive. It must have been difficult to see me that way. I remember my mom asking me so nicely if I liked where she had placed a picture. I probably answered her gruffly. The few hours it took us to complete were the first hours of no pain. I was focused and distracted. I wanted to tell my story. I gathered a photo of every person that had played a role in his life. I wanted people to look at the pictures and learn about my son. I wanted it to be the story of his life. I wanted his handsome face with all of his famous looks, especially the smirk, captured. I could have filled a thousand boards. He was my son and a brother, grandson, nephew, godchild, friend, and cousin. He played soccer, hockey and video games. He had his share of injuries. His favorite color was red, and he was famous for wearing a red, plaid shirt. I wanted people to see him happy. I was lucky to have a photo of everything I wanted to display. I was proud of that collage. When I look at the collage now, it automatically brings tears to my eyes. So many memories of Aaron are in that collage. I am glad to have it, and I await the day it brings me joy to look at it.

<u>The Story</u>

The story appeared in the newspaper two days after Aaron died. My family had decided to keep the article from me. I was discussing the fact that the story was still not in the paper. Somebody told me that it had already appeared in the paper. I asked for the story. I needed to see it. The title was "Sunday Drive Ends in Tragedy". Seeing it in ink was incredibly hard. I proceeded to read the story. The reporter did an amazing job. It was not just like every other car accident, where you see a picture of twisted metal with a few words about the accident. This story told people about Aaron and his life. It was very moving. I reached the part that described the accident: "The car flipped and he was ejected from the vehicle and died instantly." I trembled and struggled to hang on. I had no idea he was thrown from the car. I pictured him at rest behind the wheel. Now I had no image. The images I conjured up were horrifying. I had another thousand questions. How did he land? What were his injuries? Did he die right away? Was he lying in the road? How did he look? I wanted to see him sitting inside the car. I couldn't bear him lying alone in the road. Who found him? Did they touch him? I wished I had not read the story. I was also angry that I was not told the truth. Looking back, I would not have told me the truth either. It is too much information for the brain to process. The images created are devastating. The mind is a powerful tool. It can create very vivid pictures. I now feel sympathy every time I see an accident on television and the vehicle is shown. Sometimes the body is shown, covered. I was spared all of that. When I remember my son, it is not as a broken body. I see him whole. That is how every parent should see her child. My healing comes from realizing that other parents must go on with horrifying images that are real. Again I am grateful that I have been spared.

The First Messages

So many people came to my house that week. They were all kind and compassionate. However, one person spoke to me out of personal experience, and those words have stayed with me from that day forward. My sister's mother-in-law buried a child when he was fourteen months old. Although I was aware of this, I did not connect with her. This had happened so long ago that I was not personally aware of her suffering. She came to me that week and asked me one question. She said to me, "You only had your son for nineteen years. If God came to you on the day he was born and told you that he could only be yours for nineteen years, would you still have taken him? If God came to you today and told you that he could come back for only one day, would you take him?" I answered yes to both of the questions. She made me realize that I would have taken him if even for one day. I would not trade those nineteen years for anything. She only had her son for fourteen months, and I had mine for eighteen more years. Although my pain was deep and unbearable, there could be worse circumstances. I wonder if she realizes that she taught me my first lesson in recovery.

The days blend together in my memory. Some events are stamped in my mind and replay as if they happened yesterday. Other events play in my mind, but the order and day changes. I do know that I sat in the same spot on my couch all week. I have a view of the front porch. I began to notice a dragonfly constantly landing on my banister. Maybe there were dragonflies around my house before, but I do not recall seeing them. I thought that maybe I was too hurried to notice the wonders of nature. Then I would think, Is this dragonfly trying to get my attention? I thought that I must be silly, until other people noticed them as well. We were sitting by my pool trying to escape the oppressive heat. My aunt commented about the dragonfly. It was a large one that circled our table as he flew. As soon as she spoke, he landed on the edge of a glass on the table. He was positioned so that he faced me. He sat there for more than a minute. I stared at him and could see the color of his eyes. They were blue, just like Aaron's eyes! That moment impressed all of us. The dragonfly became our symbol for Aaron. We all began to see them everywhere. To this day I receive dragonflies in the form of gifts. My friends and family all have their own dragonfly stories. My aunt said to me, "It does not matter if Aaron sent the dragonfly. What matters is that every time we see a dragonfly, for the rest of our lives, we'll take a moment and remember Aaron." That was the beginning of my signs and a ray of hope.

Alyssa confided in me that week. The night that Aaron died, while she and I lay in bed together, Aaron appeared to her in the doorway of my bedroom. As she lay next to me, she turned to face the door, and Aaron was standing in the doorway. He smiled at her, told her he was sorry and said he loved her. He said goodbye to her and vanished. As she told me her story, chills raced up my spine. Her eyes spoke the truth.

I believed that he did come to her, but I wanted him to come to me. Why didn't I see him? I did not get to say goodbye to my son. I kept repeating these words. I wanted to turn the clock back; and even though the outcome would be the same, I would hug him at the door and tell him I loved him. I was obsessed with remembering the last time I had touched him or told him I loved him. If I had hugged him and loved him recently, then he would know for sure that I loved him. Most people did not understand my concern. They would assure me that he knew I loved him. That was not enough for me at that time. I needed confirmation, proof.

It was the night before the wake. I lay in bed between asleep and awake. I felt as if I was in a dream state, but I remember wondering if it were a dream. As I lay in my bed, I turned to look out the window. Aaron's face appeared right next to my face. I reached to him and touched his face. I felt the stubble of his goatee. I told him I loved him and kissed his lips. He had a scar on his lower lip, and I felt this scar. I told him I loved him and I said goodbye. He did not speak to me. In the very next moment I was looking out my window and I was awake. Was that a dream? He felt so real to me. I wondered if he heard my concerns. He came to me so that I could say what I did not get to say. I have moments when I believe he lives in another dimension and will be with me forever. I also have moments when I believe that my mind created the event to stop me from crossing the line into insanity.

Some time during the week we discussed which outfit Aaron would wear. Gary and I did not want him to wear a suit. We wanted him in a red plaid shirt. Aaron's favorite color was red, and he had an array of red plaid shirts. Someone selected a shirt and we chose to use the black pants that he wore when he was a waiter. Whenever we saw Aaron, he seemed to have those waiter pants on. Just before Friday I asked about the outfit. Someone told me that it was ironed, and they kept it downstairs away from view. I asked to see the outfit. The shirt and pants were fine, but I did not like the t-shirt that was chosen. It was a plain green shirt that matched the outfit. Aaron would never have chosen one to match so perfectly. He would typically wear a t-shirt that had a picture or saying on it. I would ask him to change to a matching shirt. He would then turn the shirt backward or inside out. He did not care about those things. This is the only time that Gary went into Aaron's room. He chose a black, Boston Bruins t-shirt. Aaron was an avid hockey fan, and he loved going to the Bruins games with my brother. We knew this shirt was perfect. We chose to have the shirt face forward. I wanted the Bruins logo to appear under the red shirt.

The Wait is Over

I awoke on this day with such anxiety. I felt as if I would jump out of my skin. This was the first day I styled my hair. I remember someone saying to me that I was finally joining the living. It did not feel right to enhance my looks. I believed from the beginning that I had to look the part of a mourner. I am not Italian, but I believed I should wear a black banner to tell the world that I had lost my son. Gary's sister bought food from Boston Market. We ate because it would be a long day. When my daughters finished getting ready, I remember how beautiful they looked to me. I was so lucky to have them. How could I be the luckiest person in the world and at the exact same time be the unluckiest person in the world? This conflict haunts me.

My husband walked to the mailbox. The day before was a holiday so there were two days of mail to gather. He is typically obsessed with getting the mail. He walked through the door with an armload of mail. There were hundred of cards, spiritual bouquets, and letters. I was amazed. We opened a few of them. I opened one and pictures of Aaron fell out. The following note was included,

"To the Zabierek Family,
We thought your family would like to have these
pictures that we took at (2) parties that we had
at Jimmy's II. We had our favorite waiter who
was a friendly funny kid. The picture with
him holding the plate is when he sang "happy
birthday to Nancy" (whose name was Ann),
which made everybody chuckle. He made that
a memorable night for us. The group picture is
at a retirement party of one of our friends (from
Raytheon). We asked him to join in our group
picture; he had become part of the "group".
We all want to say how sorry we are to hear of
your loss, and we want you to know that Aaron
(we did not know his name, we just called him
"our favorite waiter"). He will be missed by the
many people whose "night out" he made special.
Remember the good times. The girls."

I sobbed. He was a wonderful waiter. He impressed these strangers so much that they were compelled to write to me. What more can a mother ask of her child? He had a job and performed it well. I remember thinking that the waiter job was an insignificant job. I wanted him to look for a more important job. This letter was a testament that he did his job well. Isn't that what matters? That letter was a gift. I read it often, and feelings of love and pride for my son overcome me.

Our families had arrived. I could see fear mixed with the grief in their eyes. How would we handle seeing Aaron? I feared for my parents and in-laws. There are health issues with them, and I was worried that they would collapse when they saw Aaron. I have an aunt on my biological father's side that I am extremely fond of. She is my second mother. I do not have a relationship with my biological father but have remained close to her. Her son is a paramedic and her daughter married a paramedic. We chose to have our immediate families with us when we saw Aaron for the first time. I wanted plenty of people present for my daughters and parents. I also asked my aunt and her family to be present. I thought the paramedics might be needed, and they were an intricate part of Aaron's life. When we arrived at the funeral parlor, I could see them waiting for us. The same fear and grief was in their eyes.

We waited outside. The feeling is indescribable. It is like butterflies' wings batting around feverishly in your stomach. You feel as if you can't stand it. Half of me wanted to run in, and the other half wanted to go away. My dad went inside to check on a few financial matters. They took him into see Aaron. I am amazed that he went in alone. I could have never done that. He came out to tell me that he saw Aaron and that he looked good. I remember thinking, How could he look good? He was dead. My dad then gave me dreadful news. He said that because of his injuries I could not touch him. I would not accept that news. I cried and cried. All week I had waited to touch my son. I needed to touch him and tell him that I loved him. My tears and pain concerned my dad. He went back inside. A compromise was made. Gary, the girls, and I could touch him, but only his hands. I settled for that.

The time had come. "Are you ready?" I was asked. One is never ready for that next step. Gary, the girls, and I walked in arm in arm. My family followed behind. We approached the casket slowly. Aaron was lying in the casket we had chosen. It was real. This was not a dream. My beautiful boy was dead. He had his red plaid shirt on. He almost appeared to be sleeping. But he wasn't. I knelt and reached to him.

He was so cold. He did not feel like Aaron. Aaron was always warm and his hands were so soft. They were his hands, because I recognized them, but I couldn't accept it. I kept saying, "Oh, dear God. I want him back" over and over again. I was overcome. I felt hands trying to pull me away from the casket. The next memory I have is sitting in a chair surrounded by everybody. I do not remember getting into the chair. People were calling my name over and over again. They were telling me to open my eyes. Why? Where was I? I opened my eyes and again was hit with the harsh reality. Aaron really died. I felt so weak. I just wanted to sleep. I wanted to go away to a safe place and hide from the world. I couldn't so I sat there wishing an end to my pain.

Father David arrived and performed the prayer service privately. They expected so many people to attend the wake that they did not want to stop it for the prayers. At this point we asked our closest friends to join us. I don't remember the prayers. I just sat in my chair. I wanted the wake to begin so that the end would come. What would I say to people? How would I react to them? I was anxious as I sat there looking at the doors, waiting for them to open. I just wanted to close my eyes and escape. Finally, the doors opened. It was time.

The first group to enter was the staff from Jimmy's II, the restaurant where Aaron had worked. I had never met them before. I noticed immediately that they all wore a yellow ribbon with an angel pinned in the center of it. This warmed my heart. I was emotionally touched by their tribute.

The line of people did not appear to end. I never stood; I just sat in my chair. Some people would kneel beside me and some would bend over. Others could only shake my hand. I know it must have been frightening to look at me. My husband was amazing. He stood by my side and was able to speak to everyone. I kept thinking I just wanted to sleep. I would look for my daughters and be thankful that my younger sister or brother-in-law was with them. I wanted to go to them, but I was frozen in that chair and could not move. Fortunately many of their friends came to support them. I was impressed by their courage to face the girls. I am grateful that they came for my daughters and supported them through the night.

I finally had no choice and had to get out of my chair. I needed to go to the restroom. It's funny that I remember this. The word spread that "she has to use the facilities." A hustle and bustle ensued. They shut the doors to Aaron's viewing room. Our dear friend was the door guard and he monitored the people, essentially performing crowd control. Others paved the way for me to walk to the restroom. When I stood for the first time, I must have wavered because in an instant my middle sister and middle brother were at my side. My brother-in-law was behind me, as I was told. They supported me and guided me to the bathroom. I kept thinking, I can do this. Why are they holding me? I could see the people looking at me with such pity. It was as if I had left my body and could look around the room. In my head I saw everyone and wanted to speak out. My physical body restrained me from doing what I wanted. I literally needed assistance to stand and walk. On the way I faltered many times. My cousin's husband, the paramedic, came to the rescue. He kept eye contact with me and led me to the chair, while my sister and brother held me up. He stood in front of me and firmly said to me, "Debbie, look into my eyes. Debbie, look at me." He pointed his fingers at his eyes for me to focus. We must have been a sight to see. Once we arrived at the bathroom, my brother and sister took me in. When my brother turned to leave, someone had shut the door. I can still see the look of horror on his face. He was trapped in the ladies room with his two sisters! He attempted to leave the bathroom, but my sister would not let him go. I can smile about it today, but am grateful that he did that for me. How much closer can a brother and sister get? This is what family does for you in times of tragedy. All reservations are thrown aside, and caring for a loved one is a priority. My sister was very matter-of-fact and told my brother, "Just turn around". Once I was done, he insisted that I leave and return to my protective chair immediately. I disagreed with him. After all, I needed to wash my hands! He was fearful I could not stand any longer, but he relented and let me wash my hands. I tend to have a stubborn streak. He held a cold, wet cloth to my neck. They cared for me. When I think of what they did for me in that bathroom, tears of incredible love surface. I am blessed to have such compassionate people in my life. We do joke about it today. When I see my cousin's husband, he'll tell me to look into his eyes. It is funnier to joke with my brother about coming into the ladies room with me. I made the walk several times that night. I do not remember the trips. I do recall, on one subsequent trip, I saw my aunt out of the corner of my eye. I heard her say, "She shouldn't have to do this. It's not right."

I made it back to my safety net after that first trip. The doors opened and we began again. In my lifetime, I have never seen so many people in one night. It impressed me that people from every area of Aaron's life came. His soccer coach, when he was ten years old, came with his son. He said to me, "You don't remember me, do you?" I said, "I do absolutely remember you. I do not know your name, but you were my son's soccer coach and that is your son Ricky." He was surprised. He told me that he had to come because Aaron was such a great kid. He promised me that he would never forget Aaron. The night continued with such stories. Aaron's second grade teacher came. We saw old friends, co-workers and relatives that we had long since forgotten about. The outpouring of support was phenomenal. Some people had to wait up to two hours in line to see us.

There was one special moment for us, especially for my husband. As I stated earlier, Aaron attended Norwich University (NU) for one semester. NU is a military university. About six cadets came to Aaron's wake in full dress uniform. Some came from as far away as Connecticut. The first NU Cadet to arrive was Aaron's former roommate. He stopped in line and spoke to us. He appeared nervous as he spoke to us. I look back and realize that it took a tremendous amount of courage for him to see us. He explained that the fellow cadets missed Aaron. He told us that Aaron was the best Regimental Bugler that NU had. They had all expected Aaron to return. They believed once Aaron returned to NU, he would achieve the lyre award for his music. His roommate presented my husband with this award. It is a gold pin in the shape of a lyre. We were deeply moved and incredibly proud of our son. My ordinary son was proving to be very extraordinary.

The last person that came to see us was a girl the same age as Aaron. She entered the room with her mother. When I saw them, I was immediately overwhelmed. I recognized her from Aaron's elementary school. She expected me not to remember her. I did not remember her name, but I recognized her. She attended kindergarten with my son. She told her mother she had to come to the wake after she read Aaron's story in the newspaper. She said she remembered that special blonde-haired, blue-eyed little boy and wanted to pay her respects. Yes, the world is full of kind, compassionate human beings. It is moments like this that pave my road to recovery with hope.

The evening finally came to an end. The room was empty except for family and close friends. I began to look around the room and noticed so many flowers. The arrangements were so beautiful. I wanted to know who had sent each arrangement. My sister started to point to the flowers and read the cards to me. But a decision was made to take us home. It had been a very long evening. I asked to be taken to the casket to say goodbye to Aaron. It was at this point that I realized that his essence was missing. I looked at him; and although I knew that it was my son, something was missing. All the previous wakes I had attended were for older people. Those people appeared as if they were sleeping. My son was in front of me, but his soul was gone. This is when I began to question if life after death existed. If he appeared to be missing a soul, where did it go? Are we made up of more than flesh and bone? Does he still exist? Where is he? I resolved to find him in his new state. I promised myself I would search until I found him. I touched him again. I spoke the words I wished I had spoken the day he died, but never did. I believed that if his soul lived on, it was definitely in that room with me. I wanted to stay with him until the funeral. I could not. My family urged me to leave. Reluctantly, I gave in to them.

I had assistance getting into the car. I knew I was creating such a commotion. Why couldn't I just do it all on my own? The safety net of my family and friends was comforting once I let them help me. We arrived home. As they were assisting me up my front steps, I could hear them talking. My cousins were making a decision to carry me up the stairs. I had a lucid moment! I would not be carried. They would know how much I weigh! I gathered the last bit of strength and cooperated enough to walk to my bedroom. I collapsed onto the bed. Every ounce of energy was drained from me. My mother and a very dear friend actually undressed me. I was too weak. Lack of sleep and food had sapped my energy. They tucked me into my bed and left me. I shut my eyes and begged for sleep.

Saying Goodbye

I awoke with such anxiety. Grief transforms to physical pain. This day was similar to the night when we had been notified that Aaron had been killed. The eyes opened and the feet stepped on the floor. Loved ones directed me. My husband did make a decision that none of us would take any medication. He was concerned that the medication would give all of us less control. We followed his instructions. Family gathered once again. I do not remember that morning until I was sitting in a chair at the funeral parlor. I looked at my son. How could I say my final goodbye? This would be the last time I saw him or touched him in my lifetime. I wanted to hold him and never let go. I had to bury my son. I screamed inside my head. Why couldn't this be a dream? I wanted to wake up. Memories flooded me. Each one brought more intense pain. I was suffocating. Suddenly, I head a familiar sound. My daughter Ashley was crying. Her pain was as intense as mine. I called out to her. She came to me and sat on my lap. Motherly instincts took over. I held her. My fear for her became a reality. I wanted her safe. I wanted to absorb her pain. I would not lose two children. I sat with her and held her until it was time to go. God bless the funeral director. As I knelt by Aaron, he was firm with me. He said, "The longer you stay, the harder it will be for you to leave." I touched my son. I told him that I loved him to the core of my being. I kissed his lips goodbye and walked out of the room. That was absolutely the most difficult task I had done in my life. Please God, let it be the most difficult task I'll ever have to do.

We arrived at the church. I focused on my daughters and Gary. I did not see anything else around me. We chose to place the linen cloth over the casket ourselves. He was our son and he was the girls' brother. It was our responsibility to take care of him. I cry as I write this. A mom and dad should never have to perform this task. It is a miracle that we survived that moment. We walked down the aisle arm in arm, Gary, the girls, and I. At a wedding a videographer captures the memories. The day is filled with excitement and it is easy to forget the moment. No video was taken that day. I forget most of the funeral mass. I sometimes almost wish I could relive it. Maybe it will be more real to me. I have moments when it's hard to believe that it actually occurred. I recall some of Father David's eulogy. He spoke about Aaron with intense love. Not many people are fortunate to have a priest speak from personal love and admiration. Today many friends have told me that Aaron's funeral was the most beautiful funeral they have ever attended, if that is possible. Beautiful seems inappropriate, yet there is no word to describe it. My husband is an incredible person. During the week prior, he was able to plan some of the service. I was unaware of this. He requested to have a trumpet player at the church. This was something special that Aaron did, and he wanted the same done for his son. A friend coordinated the trumpet players. My husband also requested one song. As I sat in the church and the trumpet sound echoed throughout the church, it was bittersweet to me. The song played was "Eagle's Wings." The notes were beautiful and took my breath away. I envisioned two angels carrying Aaron straight to heaven.

I am grateful for my husband's courage. He did what he could to make the service special and personal. The service concluded and we were directed to leave. We held on to the girls and walked out of the church. We entered the limousine and sat in silence, tears spilling.

I saw the pallbearers putting Aaron into the car. My heart ached for them. That had to be a difficult task for them. How unfair life can be. The cruel twists it can take. A distant cousin of mine was at the wake. He had a son that was born just days apart from Aaron. The sympathy was evident in his eyes. I believe he connected because the boys were born so close in the same hospital. He is a detective with the police force in town. He offered a police escort for Aaron. He said, "Everybody that I have spoken to remarks that Aaron was a great kid. He never caused trouble. Supplying a police escort is the least we can do." He was true to his word. We had a full escort. It seemed that the entire police department was there for my son. There were many motorcycles and several police cruisers. As we drove through town, a motorcycle would race by the limousine to stop the traffic at the next intersection. It was an incredible sound to hear. As the hearse passed, the officers saluted. We thought strangers must have said, "Look at that motorcade. Somebody important must have died." Yes, one of the most important persons in the world did die. It was a proud moment for me to see those police motorcycles and cruisers. I've heard that Aaron's procession was the largest in town, with 122 cars participating. Somebody said to me, "The town of Methuen stopped to let Aaron go by." I couldn't ask for a better tribute. We thought Aaron must have looked down and said, "Wow! Look at the motorcycles! Cool!" Aaron spoke often of becoming a police officer or a state trooper. How fitting that he had this incredible tribute.

We arrived at the cemetery. I stood in disbelief. The end was here. I would say my final goodbye. My heart ached. The emptiness surrounded me. I did not notice anybody. My eyes focused on his casket. My girls today were amazed at the volume of people that stood around us. I wish I had seen the people. The service was short and I do not remember it. The silence was deafening. The air was still and thick with sadness. Suddenly the stillness was interrupted, and a familiar sound rang loud and clear. I heard a trumpet. That beautiful trumpet sounded throughout the cemetery. My heart melted. That sound was so connected to Aaron. I thought for a moment, if I turn around he'll be there! He wasn't. I would never hear his beautiful trumpet music again. Several of his friends had gathered for this music tribute. The song was Amazing Grace, and then it changed into a familiar song that I couldn't place at the time. I was to learn later that Aaron actually had requested Amazing Grace be played at his funeral. He was with friends and they were watching a tribute honoring those who lost their lives in the tragedy on September 11, 2001. Bagpipe players were playing Amazing Grace and Aaron made that comment. At the time the friends told him not to speak about his death. They remembered that conversation and had honored Aaron's request. Did my son have a sense he was not going to live long? The song played in the middle of Amazing Grace was McArthur's Park. Aaron had a solo in the marching band show his senior year of high school. His solo was from "McArthur's Park." His friends created a wonderful tribute. I couldn't have asked for a more special one. My son was loved. He was respected and well known. My ordinary boy was extraordinary.

The mercy meal was held at my uncle's American Legion Hall. He and some friends put together the meal. I sat at my table. My husband wanted to walk around and see people. I could not get out of my chair. A plate of food was put in front of me. I ate but did not taste it. People came to me. I wanted to run from that hall. I did not want it to be over. I wanted to go back to the beginning of the week. At least then there was a plan. Now what would I do? My two very best girlfriends came to me. They asked me if I wanted company at my house or did I want to be alone. I begged them to come home with me. I could not be alone. When I was alone, the pain was at its greatest. They promised not to leave me. I am blessed to have two friends who love me so much. I couldn't sit there any longer and asked to be taken home.

On the way home, I asked to drive by the accident scene. We stopped at the telephone pole. There were flowers, candles, and pictures. I saw one large frame with many pictures of Aaron. I wanted that picture frame. I could not leave it outside to be destroyed by weather. My beautiful son's pictures were in the frame, and I wanted it. My friend got out of the car and took the collage. I asked, "Can we take it?" He said, "Yes, he is your son."

We arrived home. The day passed and the emptiness increased. I thought that, maybe with the funeral over, it would be easier. I was wrong. Thankfully, some of my family came to visit. At least they could distract us. We sat by the pool and ate pizza. It tasted like nothing. I ate it because someone put it in my hand. The clock ticked and finally the day ended. Our visitors left and we were alone. We prepared for bed, hoping that sleep would overcome us. I lay in bed. This would be the worst day of my life. I buried my beautiful boy. I said goodbye. I waited in the darkness. It was over.

The Emptiness

I awoke the morning after with heaviness in my heart. What next? I
asked this question many times. I could hear activity downstairs. I
did not have the energy to get out of bed. I lay there for what seemed
like an eternity. Finally, when I heard the vacuum cleaner running, I
climbed out of my bed. My husband was dis-assembling the flower
arrangements and attempting to put the house back in order. He said
to me, "This place smells like a funeral parlor. I can't stand it any more."
He had such courage. There were so many flower arrangements. One
hundred and eight arrangements were delivered to the funeral parlor,
and an additional thirty-four were delivered to our house. I did not
have the strength to help him. Each arrangement had a card with a
name on it. Each name was connected to a relationship with Aaron that
contained a floodgate of memories. I am usually very particular about
my house. I obsess with organizing and cleaning. This was probably
the first time in my life that I did not care. I sat in silence watching my
husband. I couldn't move. Thankfully, the silence was broken when
the doorbell rang. My brother and his wife were at the door once again
with Dunkin Donut's coffee! My guardian angel must have sent them.
I needed that caffeine just to hold myself in an upright position.

Once again family and friends continued to support us. My mom and dad and my in-laws were there for us as they had been every day that week. I realize it must have been difficult for them to care for us. Although we were adults, we needed the same parenting we had received in our younger years. Probably the most difficult thing to survive in addition to losing a child is to watch your child lose your grandchild. The time passed as they sat with us and attempted to take care of our needs. I found myself sitting at the kitchen table. My mother-in-law had prepared a New England boiled dinner. My parents, sister-in-law, her partner, and my in-laws were sharing this meal together. The time was 6:45 PM. Once the clock struck 7:00 PM, it would be one week to the hour of the last time I saw my son alive. I started to experience a physical pain. My family was almost enjoying this meal and I did not want to spoil their time. I slipped away to my bedroom. It was such an ominous feeling. I believed I could not survive another moment. Taking a breath required tremendous effort. I reached for the phone and called my girlfriend. We talked for a long time. At first I watched the clock for the hour to approach. Her talking distracted me. 7:00 PM passed and nothing happened. It was as if I thought something would happen. The dread was indescribable. Yet somehow I survived that moment. My friend talked to me and took the focus away from the clock. Life becomes a game of finding things to pass the time. Today and every Sunday since that first week my husband lights a red candle from 7:00 PM to 9:00 PM. Those two hours, every Sunday, are the most difficult to face. This candle is a tribute to Aaron. We've chosen a red candle because that was Aaron's favorite color. It is almost a peaceful feeling to see that candle burning. The flame symbolizes the torch we hold in our hearts for our son.

His Room

I was compelled to continue searching Aaron's room. I began to ask the same questions again. Did I really know my son? Was he struggling in any way? I know the accident was determined to be just that, an accident. I still wondered if there was something that I could have done to prevent it. I was not ready to let go of the guilt. As a parent, a primary role is to protect your child. I believed I had failed my son. I also lost my future with my son. If there were any answers to be found, they were in his room. His room contained his life. I believed that if I could relive his life and learn every detail about him, this would take the place of the future I would not have. My husband found the courage to join me. We began to touch everything in his room. My son was a simple boy. He did not care about his material things or how his room looked. I had argued with him so many times about cleaning his room. My goal that summer had been to have his room painted and given a new, fresh look. I wanted to redecorate his room one more time. I figured he would move out in a few years, but I could not look at the messy room any longer. Sadly, I never completed that task. Ironically, Aaron did clean his room four days before he died. He did not clean it to my standards, but he did sort out all of his things.

He tossed many childhood souvenirs, leaving those items he chose to save. As we searched the room, we automatically started to separate the items. We separated the items into categories. Something to save for us. Something to save for the girls. I wanted to save everything right down to the trash in his room. My husband was more sensible than I was and able to determine what was special and what was really trash. Aaron's life was reduced to a room of memories.

Without realizing it or planning it, we sorted through his entire room. Most of the items were ordinary. However, we found several things that gave us a glimpse into Aaron's heart. My husband opened a gym bag, and to his surprise Aaron had saved every soccer shirt he owned. They ranged in size from kindergarten age to high school age. They were all together in the same bag. Each shirt is a gateway to memories of soccer games and outings. Also saved by my son was an infant sleeper. The sleeper was so tiny it was the size of Aaron's hand. My son was a big guy. In fact, "Big Guy" became the nickname my mother gave him. It warmed my heart to see that tiny outfit. It had a soccer emblem on it. I never realized that before.

I picked up a large rock from Aaron's bookcase. It had writing on it that said, "Dog River 8/27/01." This item opened a door to the past. When Aaron attended Norwich University, he participated in Rook Week. This was the first week of school, and the students went through a boot camp experience. This was very difficult for Aaron because he was not in physical shape. He struggled that week, and at the end of the week he faced his biggest challenge. The name of the challenge was Dog River Run. The Rooks had to run a course through a river. A documentary was made from that group of students. We received a copy, and Aaron had a cameo appearance. My husband and I still not have been able to view it again since Aaron died. The scene of the drill sergeant screaming at Aaron moves us to tears. He is responding, but the emotion on his face shows that he is having a difficult time. That moment is most likely one of the most difficult moments in his life. He sheds a tear and his lip quivers as he responds to the drill sergeant. When I first watched this video, Aaron had already left Norwich. Had he still been a student at the University, I might have gone to the school to check on his wellbeing. Aaron did complete that Dog River Run. His entire corps was proud of him. That was one of the proudest moments for my husband and me. The courage and determination it took for Aaron to survive that week was amazing. The rock was our link to his military experience, and we were grateful to have it. Did Aaron realize that a simple rock from the river would become a cherished item?

The last item that surprised me in his room was a box labeled "Emily Box." This box contained all of the items Aaron's one true love, Emily, gave had given him. He saved all of her gifts and all of the notes she had written to him. This girl held a place in my son's heart. A place that would never be filled with another. That was the moment that I realized my son had experienced love even though he had lived a short life. One believes that if true love is never found life is not lived to the fullest. Knowing that he experienced true love relieved me of concern that he would miss so many wonderful moments in life. He experienced more than some would at an old age. This box also contained six dried roses. I was to learn later that Aaron made a pact with Emily. Valentine roses, that Aaron had sent Emily, were dried. Each of them saved six roses. Aaron and Emily agreed that these would be kept forever; and if one of them died, the other would place the roses in the casket. Emily approached my husband the day of the funeral and asked permission to place something in the casket with Aaron. Gary granted permission to Emily. As I said goodbye to my son, I saw roses lying on his body. Emily had saved her roses. They both had saved the roses. If Aaron was indeed watching, he saw that his love was indeed reciprocated. I hoped that my son knew this when he was alive.

Many people have asked us how we accomplished the task of cleaning out his room. I do not have an answer. If I had gone into that room with the intention of cleaning it out, I might not have been able to do it. My reason was different. I was searching.

It became a healing process for me to do that room. I found my answer. Aaron had no secrets from us. He was simply the Aaron that we knew and loved. He did not lead a secret life. There were no letters speaking about hidden pain. I learned that my son was loving and compassionate and sentimental. He was not an ordinary boy. This, combined with his friend's assurance that Aaron was on top of the world, strengthened my belief about the accident. It was just an accident. In believing that, the guilt subsided. I had no control over his actions that day. There was nothing I could have done to stop it from happening. I would repeat this to myself each time, convincing myself more and more.

We made a decision, as a family, on what to do with his room. My girls shared a room. Alyssa asked for Aaron's room, while Ashley stated that she still could not enter the room. It made sense to us to give Alyssa the room. The girls were getting older and needed their privacy. Ironically, I had wished for a spare room in the past. I thought my house was not big enough. I wanted more room. Suddenly, I had an extra room. It did not matter. My house could have been the size of a mansion, and it would not have mattered. My children and my husband mattered. I would have lived in a one-room shack if I could have my son back. My priorities began to shift. We all agreed that Alyssa would have his room. As we sorted through Aaron's things, I selected a book from his bookcase. Alyssa had come into the room. I opened the book and a bookmark fell out of it. It was a souvenir card that had the name Alyssa and the meaning of the name. Alyssa said, "Hey, how did Aaron get that card? Why did he have it?" My husband said, "Alyssa, he is giving you his approval. He is saying that you are meant to have his room." We all sat still for a moment. My husband's words comforted all of us. I don't know how the card ended up in Aaron's book, but we consider it another sign from Aaron.

Return to Work?

Gary had been with his current employer for only three months when Aaron died. His employer was very supportive and gave him permission to take as much time as he needed. After we buried Aaron, he decided to take an additional week before returning to work. He felt obligated to return to work because he was a new employee. He did not want to take advantage of his employer. When he did return, the first few days were very difficult. Each day he only lasted until noon. Many people would say to us, "Stay out as long as you need to." We would ask, "What about the bills?" We still had two other children to support and a home to maintain. Unfortunately, we did not have access to a plush bank account.

I knew that I also had to return to work, but could not imagine going back at all. My company offered two weeks bereavement time for the loss of an immediate family member. I understand that business must continue, but how could I possibly recover enough to return in two weeks? My girls were on summer vacation, and the thought of leaving them horrified me. If they had to be home to face the memories, then I had to be there for them. Fortunately, I did have more than eight weeks of sick time. I believed without a doubt that my company would allow me to use my sick time for this reason. My husband took the assignment of contacting my company. Although they were just as supportive as my husband's employer, there was a snag to utilizing my sick time. I realize now that my company had guidelines to follow. However, when my husband called, they stated that in order to use my sick time, I had to take a medical leave. To be approved for this leave, a physician's note was required.

Almost immediately after Aaron died, I expressed the desire for my husband and me to see a counselor. I told my family, "I have seen all of those Life Time movies. I know that families fall apart after such a loss. I am determined to save the remainder of my family." The mother instinct was strong, and I needed to protect my family. My mother in-law arranged for an appointment with a counselor for Gary and me. We decided to see the counselor without the girls for the first visit. We saw the councilor during the second week after Aaron died. It was one of the difficult moments for me. Basically Gary and I had to relive the prior week. As I recall the visit, I do not know how we got through it. I remember two facts given to us. The first one was that our grief was too raw. We were told that it would take at least one year to begin to recover. We had to survive all of the "firsts" before moving on. The second fact was that, of the marriages that suffered the loss of a child, only 10% survived. This harsh fact frightened me. I did not know if my daughters or I could survive this additional loss. I made a commitment to protect my marriage and my children at all costs.

The counselor gave me a note to stay out of work due to depression. Imagine that? I was depressed. Who wouldn't be? However, my employer would not accept a note from the counselor. They required a note from a physician. My husband called my primary care physician. Her staff indicated that she could not write the note because she was not treating me for depression. My husband was angry. I remember family members offering assistance, but my husband was determined to resolve the issue. At everyone's recommendation, he spoke directly to my doctor. She sympathized with my situation and agreed to write the note. My employer accepted the note. I was relieved. I did not have to face the challenge of the working world for the remainder of the summer. Once again, I thanked God for my husband.

His Memorial

The last step in completing the process of burying our child was for my husband and me to select a headstone for the grave. I wanted to get the stone because I believed it would complete his resting-place. I wanted it finished. I thought that by finishing the grave I could close that chapter of my life and move on. My parents took us to the local monument shop. I had no idea what the process was in selecting a stone. I pictured a typical gray stone seen at most cemeteries. I expressed my desire to have Aaron's stone stand out among the rest. I revisited my concerns that Aaron would be lost in a sea of gray stones. Ideally I wanted a six-foot black marble stone. My son was tall and stood out in every crowd he was in. When he marched in the band, he could be spotted quickly. I was proud to see him marching in his uniform, and I wanted to duplicate that feeling in the cemetery.

We arrived, and one of the owners assisted us. My husband and I were still very fragile. He was incredibly compassionate. I realize that dealing with survivors is his job, but he did that difficult task with ease. He took us into a private room. He led us on an incredible journey. The questions he asked were not what I thought would be asked. I assumed we had to select size and color only. After expressing his sympathy, he asked us to talk about Aaron. His vision was to create a memorial about our son. The stone should represent Aaron's life. Most of the comments came from my husband once again. The first statement made was that Aaron's name meant "High Mountain." The stone evolved from there. We decided to chisel a mountain out of a block of black granite. The director took an actual picture of Mount Washington, in New Hampshire, for the artist to use as a guide when chiseling the stone. He was not aware that Aaron had intended to climb Mount Washington in August of 2003. He had hung a slip of paper on the refrigerator with the following, 50P3MMT. It was Aaron's code to state that when he lost 50 pounds he would climb Mount Washington in three months. Was this yet another coincidence, or was this a sign from Aaron? We never mentioned a specific mountain to the Memorial Director. The granite would be black as I requested. At that point, we talked about Aaron's hobbies and favorite things. The director suggested a silhouette of Aaron at the bottom of the mountain. There would be a road leading to the top of the mountain. This would represent Aaron's journey on the road to heaven. Aaron's silhouette would be playing the trumpet. Musical notes would drift from the trumpet and scatter around him. Sitting on the top of the mountain would be a cross with radiating light to symbolize heaven. He further amazed us by suggesting that we place stars around the name Zabierek to symbolize the girls, Gary, and me. I was deeply touched with his creation. We selected the phrase "God's Creation" to be displayed at the bottom of the mountain. These were the words Aaron spoke on that trek up the mountain with Father David.

We were moved to a different room to watch the director bring the stone to life on the computer. As he created the stone, he made some additional changes. The section of the stone that would be chipped away to make the mountain was recessed. The top layer of granite was removed to reveal a gray shade of stone. This is where the name was placed. The name remained in black, shiny granite. It appeared dignified against the black. The scattered stars shone brightly. The back of the stone read "Our Son and Guardian Angel" with the dates of his birth and death. On one side of the inscription was a soccer ball, and the other side contained a hockey player. These were two of Aaron's favorite things. The finished product is absolutely amazing. He managed to capture every essence of Aaron on that stone. The stone is a true memorial to my son's life.

When we drive into the cemetery, the stone can be seen from a long distance. I accomplished my goal. Aaron stands above the crowd once again.

Thank You

It had only been a week and a half since Aaron's death. I was compelled to thank everybody that helped and sent a gift. My goal was to fill my time with a project. As long as I was occupied, there was no time for thinking. I arranged for all the women in my life to come over and write the thank-you cards. This was a vast undertaking. I became the same possessed woman that I was when I made the collage. How lucky I am to have so many people love me. I picture the scene of us sitting around the table with cards, lists, address books, etc. What a sight we must have been. Everybody was patient with me and did a wonderful job. The thank-you cards had a spot for the name of the deceased individual. I used to address wedding invitations in calligraphy. I insisted to write my son's name in calligraphy. I must have written his name three hundred times. I had always dreamed that I could address his wedding cards in calligraphy. A twist of fate had me addressing thank-you cards for his funeral.

I remember telling my friend a little story to help her console her sister when she lost her husband. Life is like taking a walk down a long corridor. This corridor is lined on each side with many doors. All of the doors appear to be the same. One must proceed down the corridor

56

and enter each room approached. As each door is opened and the room entered, the contents of the room are revealed. One room may be filled with happiness. Another filled with pain. However, there is one door that opens to a room filled with blackness and enough sadness to fill an ocean. Some people are spared from entering this room. Although there is a door leading out of the room, it must be entered by those select few. There is no telling how long one is in the room. We, supporting our loved one, must remember that there is an exit to the room. Eventually our loved one will come back out. I found myself thinking of this story as I addressed the thank-you cards. I was in that black room. Where was the exit door? Would I ever find it?

More Messages From Aaron

I spent any quiet moments reading the John Edward book. One prominent theme throughout the stories told by John was that loved ones who passed over sent signs from Heaven to those on earth. These signs were various messages about things special to the one who passed. These messages could be connected to the loved one by their family. The messages can be sent in a variety of ways. A familiar song on the radio or a physical item being noticed is a common sign sent. There are even instances where an item may be moved to alert the attention of a family member. Prior to this time in my life, I had never heard anyone speak of signs from loved ones who passed on. When I lost a grandparent, although I was sad, I was never devastated. This time it was different. I wanted to know if the other side existed. Where did Aaron go? How could I get proof? I believed if I received signs, I would have confirmation that there was another side to this world. My other option was to believe that Aaron had died and that was the end of it. Or I could believe that life continued in some form and Aaron existed in a place where I could not see him. I chose to believe the latter. I wanted some proof of this afterlife. I needed to believe that my son lived on. If Aaron gave me a sign, I would have the proof I desired. The trumpet was a symbol for Aaron, so it was natural for me to ask for a trumpet. I immediately began asking Aaron for signs. I would look to the sky and say, "All right Aaron, you know about this John Edward stuff. Send me a sign. I want a trumpet. Aaron, please send me a trumpet. I need to know that you are still alive somewhere else. I need to know if you are happy." I must have said this ten times a day. I became obsessed. If Aaron did exist on the other side, I was driving him crazy!

Suddenly I began to receive trumpet signs. These first signs were to be the beginning of many to come. When we cleaned Aaron's room, I found a case with rolls of film. My daughter took the film to be developed. One roll was from Aaron's stay at Norwich. Many of the pictures were of his friends, people we did not recognize. However, there was one amazing picture. Aaron was dressed in fatigues and sitting in the chapel. He was holding his trumpet. A friend must have taken this picture of him. It is a beautiful picture of Aaron with his trumpet! Aaron is smiling, and in most pictures he chooses not to smile. My daughter came home with the pictures and told me, "Mom, he sent you a trumpet! Aren't you happy?" I do cherish that picture. However, as most people who know me would agree, I am a "glass half empty" kind of woman. I thought that maybe this was a coincidence. My family disagreed with me. Aaron had that film for the past year and had already developed it. He would have shown us the picture, but he didn't. It was more than a coincidence that we saw it for the first time immediately after his death. He not only gave me a sign, but he was smiling as if to say, "I'm okay Mom."

There were two more strong signs that week. Ashley received a call from the photo lab. They were relocating and apparently found a role of developed film that was never picked up by Ashley. She had taken black and white pictures of her friends for her photography class. She must have forgotten about the film. An employee found the pictures in a drawer while packing. The entire roll was pictures of Ashley's friends, except one picture. This picture was of Aaron. The shot is from the shoulders up. He is standing in the kitchen, and it is almost a profile shot. What makes the picture incredible is that Aaron is clearly laughing out loud in the picture. It is an amazing picture of my son. Because he is standing in front of an old refrigerator, we were able to determine that the picture is at least one year old. Ashley does not remember taking this picture of Aaron. Once again my daughter reminded me that I was given a sign with a message from Aaron. He was happy. Was it a coincidence that the photo lab relocated two weeks after my son's death? Was it a coincidence that the film was never picked up or found?

The most prominent trumpet sign came at the end of that second week. It was Sunday and the day took a long time to pass. I was lying on the couch as usual. My husband insisted that I needed to get out of the house. He attempted to call my parents but they were not home. He tried a friend, but she had company, and I would not go to her house with strangers present. He suggested calling my aunt. I told him, "Call her and if she is home, I will go. However, if she is not home, that's it. I'm staying home." Fortunately, she was home and we ventured out. Curiously a dragonfly was sitting on the windshield of the car. We stopped at a light and a dragonfly flew in front of the car. It appeared to me that dragonflies were trying to get my attention. This was the third instance where I noticed a dragonfly in an unusual circumstance. Was Aaron showing me these dragonflies? I wanted to believe Aaron was with us. We arrived at my aunt's house. She has an apartment with my cousin. His wife was home, and we visited with my aunt and cousin's wife. My cousin's wife is very interested in the spirit world. We had an open discussion about this topic. I reiterated to them about my request to Aaron for a trumpet. We visited for a while and then returned home. My husband was right to take me out for a visit.

The change brightened my mood and helped pass the time. The next morning I received a call from my aunt. She had been sleeping in and was startled awake to the sound of a trumpet! She has never heard a trumpet being played in the neighborhood before; someone in the neighborhood was practicing the trumpet! She and my cousin's wife were amazed and convinced that Aaron was sending me a message. When she called me, I had goose bumps all over. It was a nervous tingling feeling. Yet I could only think, "Why didn't I hear a trumpet?" My aunt believed that Aaron utilized what was available to him. There wasn't a trumpet player in my neighborhood. She also believed that maybe I could not handle such a prominent sign. She and my cousin's wife were confident that Aaron was not only an extraordinary boy, but he was becoming an extraordinary spirit. My faith was strengthening, but I had many, many set backs. I would shout, "I don't care if there is another world with him alive in it! I want him in my world, or I want to join him!" If he did exist, surely he would reach out to me in a powerful way.

Another sign discussed in the book was that occasionally a spirit would appear to their loved one. Alyssa saw her brother the night he died. She did not tell my husband or me for fear we would not believe her. As I talked about the book and spirit world, it opened a door of communication for her. She shared her moment. It happened when she and I were lying in the bed attempting to escape into sleep. She remembers looking at me and thinking that I had fallen asleep. She rolled over and faced the door. Aaron appeared to be standing in the doorway. He was transparent, but she could clearly see his face. He waved to her, smiled, and said," Alyssa, I'm sorry, I love you; goodbye." He threw her a kiss and vanished. It happened in a split second. She believes with all of her heart that Aaron came to say goodbye to her. As she told me her story, I could see love and certainty in her eyes. Alyssa has been a rock for our family. She is certain that Aaron lives on and watches over all of us. Her attitude reminds me of Aaron. She has said many times that we must have faith and believe that Aaron is in a better place watching over us. There were times when I was depressed and Alyssa would say to me, "Mom, sit up. Please smile for me, Mom. Everything will be okay." She didn't like to see me lying on the couch so often. She would tell me that Aaron would not want me to be so sad. I have to believe Aaron visited her that night. He chose Alyssa because of her open mind and heart. He knew she would receive him more easily than the rest of us.

My mother-in-law also received a sign from Aaron. I did not learn of the sign until much later in time, but I believe it was at this point that she actually received the sign. She was in that state just prior to sleep. Aaron appeared to her with a tall man dressed in green robes. She believes that he was with a priest. She was comforted by this sign. The pastor of our church had passed away prior to Aaron's death, and we believed that maybe Aaron was with him in heaven.

I wanted to see my son. I wanted one last time with him. As I struggled to cope, I just wanted to turn back the clock. I began to wish I could repeat his last day. I would hug him and tell him I loved him. It was important for me to know that he believed I love him. People would respond to my concerns by telling me I was silly to think such things. "Of course, Aaron knew that you loved him," they would tell me. Sometimes that would make me angry. My head believed them, but my heart did not. My first fear was to wonder if he knew that I loved him. I did not want people to minimize my worries. I even began to wish that if I couldn't have Aaron back, I wanted to repeat the wake and funeral. I would look at him longer and touch him more. During that time I lived each day by marking it off my imaginary calendar. As I crossed out a day, it brought me closer to the day I would see Aaron again. Instead of wanting to live longer and being afraid to die, I longed for the time I would cross over to heaven. I would look in the mirror and think, only thirty-five years to go before I see Aaron.

I lay in bed one night. My eyes were closed and I began to drift into sleep. I felt a breeze pass over very close to my face. I thought my husband had come into the room and was leaning over me. I opened my eyes and no one was there. I turned to the doorway. The room was very dark. My eyes were drawn to the ceiling near the doorway. I saw a face. It appeared to be a cherub; however, there was something familiar about this cherub. The cherub smiled and then turned away. I could see wings in back and it appeared that the cherub flew up into the sky. I was dazed. I believed I must have crossed the line to insanity. I shut my eyes and wished for darkness. The morning came quickly. I opened my eyes and had that moment of peace. I turned and faced the picture of Aaron that I had placed on my nightstand. At once I recognized the cherub. It was Aaron's face! He had posed as a cherub with the same expression in my favorite picture. I didn't care at the moment if anyone believed me. It did not matter. I climbed one more step on the ladder of my journey of faith.

Although Alyssa and I were the first to have an Aaron experience, Ashley also had a very moving experience with Aaron. He appeared to her in a dream. She awoke one morning and rushed to tell us about her amazing dream. Her eyes were bright and her face filled with love as she told her story. She was in her room. She knew in her dream that Aaron had died. He entered the room. She asked him what he was doing. He said, "I came to visit with you." She said, "But you can't. You're gone." He replied, "I know, Ashley. Don't you know that they let me leave Heaven to visit with you? I can visit you in your dreams." He sat next to her and put his arm around her. He kissed her and told her that he loved her. He then said, "I have to go now. I will come back and visit again in your dreams, because that is how I can see you now." He vanished. She said that she could feel his goatee and smell his cologne. It was very real to her. She had never had a dream with such clarity before. I do believe that my son visited my daughter. The pain on her face had momentarily disappeared. She had a look of peace and hope. I had requested proof of the afterlife and I was receiving answers.

My family has each dealt with this pain in their own way. My eldest daughter has begun to write poetry. She created a poem the night after Aaron's funeral. The poem is absolutely beautiful. She submitted the poem for publishing, and it was accepted to publish. My husband and I are incredibly proud of her. I would like to share this poem…

"A Poem For The One I Lost"

As I sit here and think of you,

I begin to grow blue.

Not long ago I could feel your touch,

Never thought I would miss you this much.

I know you're all around,

In the air and on the ground.

The raindrops are your loving tears,

The wind is you blowing away my fears.

The sunshine is your warm smile,

You can see it for miles.

You're looking down on me,

Seeing all that you can see.

While I sit or simply pace,

I somehow feel your warm embrace.

But now I must say goodnight,

And know that I love you with all my might.

My brother, my friend, my angel Aaron.

Changes

There are three bedrooms in our house. I imagined Alyssa living in Aaron's room. Although I was happy with my decision, I didn't like that there was one obvious change. So I decided that my husband and I would switch rooms with Ashley. Our bedroom had been recently redecorated, but it did not matter. I believed that if all three rooms were different, it would not be so obvious. It seems silly to me to think that changing rooms would ease the pain of Aaron's void. However, we decided to change all rooms, and I am glad we made that decision. I made it my mission to have all rooms redone within a two-week period. It was not easy to duplicate my new room; however, the distraction was a welcome one. My girlfriend and my mom helped me with the rooms during the day. If I focused on the rooms, I did not think. I could not have done it without my mother or girlfriend.

In order to begin the work on the rooms, we had to go out and purchase paint and supplies. My husband insisted that I go to the hardware store with him. I went reluctantly. I thought the 'do it yourself store' would be a safe place for me. I had a fear of encountering someone who did not know about the death of my son. How would

I react when I had to break the news? This was a great fear of mine. As we walked up and down the aisles, people were all around me. I began to panic. How could they behave so normally when I was in such despair? I wanted to shout to them, "How can you go about your business? Do you know what happened to me?" As we waited in the paint line, I was overwhelmed with panic. I needed to leave the store. My husband suggested that I leave the store and wait in the car for him, but I couldn't walk out of the store on my own. We had to complete our purchase. I was stuck in that line. When we finished our purchases, I could not leave the store fast enough. I was pushing the carriage. As I walked in the parking lot, I broke down in tears. I did not want to go on. I stopped in my tracks and just cried. Something then touched my arm. I was surprised and turned to see who had approached me. There was no one there. I looked for a bird nearby or insect and could not find any. I was brought back to reality and walked to my car. I told my husband what had happened. We wondered if Aaron had attempted to comfort me. Gary's perspective was that it pulled me out of my episode. We wanted to believe that Aaron was trying to connect with us.

My husband and I also had another amazing encounter. We were driving home from another outing to obtain supplies. The time in the car was most difficult. We thought of Aaron and did not usually speak. I was still insisting that Aaron send me trumpet signs. I asked for these signs on a daily basis. Something in the sky caught my eye. It was a cloud formation. I stared at the cloud and an angel began to take shape. I could clearly see this angel, and she was holding a trumpet. I could not believe my eyes. I pointed this out to my husband. He saw the same angel. This angel stayed in the sky for at least a mile. When we took the ramp off the highway, the car stopped and the angel was right in front of the car. We definitely were not imagining this. The comfort that we felt was peaceful and healing. Aaron sent me a trumpet. Some may want to believe that we created this angel; however, the story continues. A friend happened to travel that road the same day that we did. She had her four children in the car with her. She called me that week to tell me about the most amazing thing she and her children had seen in the sky. She described the same angel cloud. All of her children saw the same thing. As I write this today, I am filled with emotion. My son did send me a sign. I was one more step closer to believing that he lived on. He was my extraordinary boy.

Getting Back to Life

Alyssa had signed up for a summer camp at Northern Essex College prior to Aaron's death. The camp started the third week after he died. Gary was back at work. How would Alyssa get there? I had to drive her. I was terrified. It was as if I had been in the accident and could not get behind the wheel. Gary was understanding of my problem, and we both drove her the first day. It was strange to be out in the world again. Entering the college was especially difficult. We sat in the auditorium with the other children and parents. I happened to sit near a boy who looked like a young Aaron. It was incredibly difficult to control my emotions while I sat there. I asked my son to give me strength. I wanted to sob, but I could not expose these innocent people to my pain. After all, the majority were happy children. They were excited to be in a college and were giggling and behaving like children. They were so innocent. I looked at the group and wondered if they would all grow up to be adults. I wondered if any would die like my son. Did someone see me with Aaron when he was a boy and think the same thought? I looked at every child, wondering if his life would be robbed. Is this how I would spend my life? Would I have this inner struggle, to stay composed, every day? Would I ever look at a child again without wondering if he would die?

The second day came too fast. I had to drive Alyssa myself. The trip to the college was not so bad. Alyssa was with me and she distracted me. The drive home was another story. As I sat behind the wheel, I recreated Aaron's accident. I did not know how his accident had occurred, but I could imagine it. Unfortunately, this included how he landed in the road. I wanted to know the details. I could not focus on my driving. At times I could not see the road through my tears. I should not have driven that day. At one point I thought that if I just made a sharp turn, just like Aaron, I would crash and it would all end. Fortunately, a side of me was rational and kept control. I made it home without really remembering the trip. At least I drove myself for the first time. I was told that my life would be filled with many first times. When your child is born, his first year is filled with many "first events". The days are quickly counted to the first full night of sleep, the first step, and the first word. All of which bring incredible joy. When your child dies, the first year is also filled with many "first events." The days are ominously counted to the first holiday, the first birthday, and the first family moment with the void. All of which bring incredible pain. At least that day I got through a first time.

The next day Gary, Ashley, and I drove together to pick Alyssa up at the college. The three of us arrived early and decided to go into the lobby to sit and wait for Alyssa to finish. As we entered the lobby, Gary headed to a set of empty chairs to sit on. I told him that I would rather sit on the other side of the lobby so that we could see Alyssa as she came into the lobby. He begrudgingly agreed to join me. He approached the seats, and to his surprise a dragonfly was sitting on one of the chairs. He showed Ashley and me the dragonfly. As he pointed to it, he put his finger on the seat. The dragonfly moved and climbed onto his finger! We were amazed. We had never seen a dragonfly sit on someone's finger. With tears in his eyes, Gary walked to the door and let the dragonfly fly outside. As I watched my husband walk back to me, I knew we had an extraordinary son.

Another first time that stands out in my mind is the trip to the grocery store. As the days passed, some normal activities began again as well. The funeral food, as we called it, was beginning to run out. I desperately needed some groceries. Gary was working during the day, and at night he was working on redecorating the bedrooms. It made sense that I go to the store. I had the entire day before me and had the time to go. However, I would not go out in public alone. I agreed to make the trip but only if Alyssa came with me. She had two friends over for a visit and they all agreed to go with me. We arrived at the store, and the panic began to set in. Alyssa could see the frightened look in my eyes. She immediately separated the list and thought we could shop faster if she took half. I could not be left alone. Today I can laugh at her response to my situation. She said to her friends, "Which one of you wants to stay with my mom so the other two of us can shop?" One of her friends said without hesitation, "I will." It's not every day that you can tell your friends that you babysat a forty-two year old! I am amazed at the maturity of my own daughter and her friends. It's proof that people do rally at times of tragedy. How blessed I am that these teenagers rallied.

<u>*Connecting*</u>

As each day passed, my feeling of isolation intensified. I did not belong. My friends and family members were mothers, but they did not go through what I did. I had the desire to connect to someone who had suffered the same loss as I had. My girlfriend suggested that I take a day trip with her to the Cape to visit her sister. She did not lose a child; however, she lost her young husband. This was as close as I would get. In addition, Keith and Aaron were very similar. They were compassionate guys, had the same body type, and had similar goatees. Aaron was fair-haired and Keith was dark-haired, yet they could have been brothers. Keith is also the one who introduced Aaron to the afterlife. I wanted to learn more about the connection to Aaron and Keith and the afterlife. I agreed to go with my friend.

It was difficult to leave my family. I became more anxious as we drove farther away from home. There were times that I thought I would jump out of my skin. The purpose of my trip kept me from turning back. When we arrived and I connected with Heidi, it was like coming home after being away on a very long trip. We hugged and felt each other's pain. Her eyes portrayed what I had been feeling the last three weeks. One of the first things she said to me was, "When I think of my Keith and your Aaron, I believe God must be building an army." I felt an immediate bond with her, and the isolation slipped away. I belonged. We spent the afternoon visiting. We cried and shared our fears and worries.

The subject of signs was discussed. Heidi was looking for signs. She said, "I want concrete proof that the afterlife exists." I was glad she said that because I felt the same way. We wanted to know for sure that our guys lived on in a better place. If heaven did exist, we would be comforted with the fact that their lives weren't lived in vain. I brought her a gift. I had painted a picture of a yellow rose. I did this painting in a class that I take weekly. I was not excited about painting it and did not know what to do with it. It was the last item I finished before Aaron died. I chose to give this to Heidi, and the night before my trip I mounted and framed it. When she opened her present, she gasped and said, "Keith always bought me yellow roses." Through me, Keith sent her a sign. She hadn't received many signs, yet this was a powerful one. I described Aaron's service to Heidi, and she became excited about a sign she received from Aaron. She and her mother had heard the song "McArthur's Park" on the radio several times. She heard it so often that she commented about it to her mother! Through Heidi, Aaron sent me a sign. This song has new meaning for us today. I believe that Aaron and Keith are connected beyond the physical world. It could not be a coincidence that they died the same way so close together. It was also not a coincidence that we each received a sign through the other. They brought us together from beyond and were sending messages. Heidi also told me about a close friend of hers that had received a vision of Keith. It was the night he died, and she was on her way to see Heidi. Keith appeared to her in the car. Heidi believed that Keith brought her friend to her. These signs and the vision were added to my list of evidence to prove, without a doubt, that heaven existed. Suddenly

Alyssa's vision had more meaning. Could this all be true? Was this my concrete proof? I began to believe, yet I wanted more.

I did learn a valuable lesson that day. Heidi was alone. When she lost her husband, she lost her life and purpose of it. She had no children. Her house was empty. I did not have an empty house. I still had my husband to comfort me, and I had two beautiful daughters. My family needed me. I had three reasons to get out of bed in the morning. As I compared myself to Heidi, although our losses were similar, I was more fortunate than her. This became one of my tools of healing. As the saying goes, there is always someone worse off than you are. When I am feeling low, I tell myself to think of the people who may be in a more difficult situation than me. This has helped me on my road to recovery.

Getting Away

Gary, the girls, and I had plans to go to New York for a mini vacation the week after Aaron died. Needless to say, we cancelled the trip. We decided to find a place for the four of us to get away. I wanted to choose a spot that we had not visited as a family. I thought that if we went somewhere new, I could escape my grief. There would be no memories associated with the trip. We wanted to make new memories for the different family that we were. I longed for happiness for my family. We chose Old Orchard Beach in Maine. Several years earlier we had camped in that area with my in-laws, but we had not visited the beach or the center. Initially we could not find an available hotel room, but after persistence Gary did locate a condo suite. The girls were excited about going on a trip and staying in the condo. Gary and I felt we had made the right decision to get away.

We arrived at the beach. The air was fresh and the hotel was beautiful. At first it almost felt wonderful. I fooled myself into thinking that I had left the pain in Methuen. I believed that we had escaped the grief. There was a minor reprieve from the pain. It did not last very long. As we were moving our things into the suite, we took many trips on the elevator. On one trip as we walked into the hotel, I could smell a strong scent of cologne. Instantly, I was reminded of Aaron. We got on the elevator and the scent followed us. My husband and my daughters did not smell this cologne. I thought this was odd. It had to be a sign from Aaron. Why wouldn't they smell it too? Was he sending me a sign? Was he with us? Then the pain reared its ugly head. I didn't want Aaron in the form of a scent; I wanted him to be alive and with us. I was sad once more.

Don't misunderstand me, we did have some pleasurable moments, but the pain was there every step of the way. As we walked on the beach, every little boy had blonde hair and blue eyes. We dined in a fancy restaurant; and the music playing, as we were seated, was a chorus of trumpets. I remember sitting in the living room watching a movie with Gary and the girls, and I noticed a white butterfly on the balcony. My sister told me that an ancient Indian belief states that every time a white butterfly is around it means that the soul of a loved one who passed away is nearby. The butterfly on the balcony wasn't just there for a moment. It was very big and bright white. It flew by the window many times. It caught my attention because it was dark out and the butterfly was very noticeable. I imagined Aaron being with us again.

The most impressive sign came the third day of our trip. The first night we had taken a drive in search of a restaurant. We took the wrong direction because we drove for a half-hour and did not find one appealing restaurant. I wanted to find a typical beach seafood restaurant. We were disappointed that we couldn't find one and ended up dining in the hotel. That third day we took a trip to Old Port and did some shopping. Should I mention that everywhere we went we saw dragonflies in one form or another?

Alyssa was our tour guide. She had visited Old Orchard the week earlier with a friend and her family. Alyssa is very observant. She remembers every route she has ever taken. She was guiding Gary back to the hotel. She must have been talking and missed a sign because Gary took a turn and she became very excited. She wanted him to turn back because we were heading in the wrong direction. He saw a sign for Old Orchard and trusted it. He did not turn back. On that road we passed a typical beach seafood restaurant. It looked like a place that we all wanted to eat at, and we agreed to go the following night. The next night, when we walked in the door, Gary and I were overcome with a feeling of deja vu. We had been to that very restaurant with my in-laws and the kids on that camping trip. It was a place that we visited with Aaron. I was trying to escape, and Aaron was not letting me. We would have never found that restaurant if Gary had not taken the wrong turn. Was it a sign from Aaron? I learned another valuable lesson. I could run, but I could not hide.

We spent a day sitting on the beach. It was a time of reflection for me. I had been writing in a journal. Someone suggested to me that I write down my feelings. As time passed, I could look back on my writing and see my progress. How would I ever progress? I could not imagine the future without Aaron. As I wrote that day on the beach, I was inspired to write a poem. This poem describes the journey I was taking. I will share it with you:

<u>*My Lost Son*</u>

I gaze over the sea of deep blue,
My heart aches for you,
Are you out there or all around me,
Lingering beside or hovering over the sea?

I'm told you go on happy as can be,
How without the girls, Dad or me?
A pure, loving, peaceful magnificent place,
Knowing we'll join to see your face.

If a mother could wish for her son,
This life of beauty with no harm done,
She'd send the child right away,
For in pure love he'd be sure to stay.

But to choose for us to be apart,
I'd never allow for my broken heart,
The pain, sadness and emptiness I endure,
The tears through everything I see are a blur.

The memories, the joy you brought to my life,
Enhancing the role I had as a wife,
To imagine you not ever being with me,
Is a path in life I can't remotely see.

So I'll look to the future with those I love,
Knowing you'll shine on us from above,
Someday we'll join in a warm embrace,
I'll hold, caress and kiss your loving face.

Aaron's Image

When we returned from vacation, I developed the film. As usual, I was prompt in developing the film, but there were pictures from Alyssa's dance recital included in the roll. I try to be organized, but considering the events that had unfolded, I am not surprised that I had some old pictures on the film. When I received the pictures back, I forgot that I had asked Alyssa to take a picture of the accident site. Those pictures were included in the film. I was shocked and amazed at what I saw. Alyssa took four pictures of the site. Two were from across the street, one was very close up to the telephone pole, and the other picture was of the back of the telephone pole. All four pictures had a golden image in the center. This image is the shape of a person's head and shoulders! The remaining pictures on the roll of film, both pictures before and after this group, were normal photos. The angle of the sun is coming in from the left side of the pictures and therefore is not the cause of the glow in the center of the pictures. The same halo is in the pictures of the front and the back of the telephone pole. We have come to believe that the golden halo is actually Aaron's aura. I have had some ghost hunting experts view these pictures and the negatives. These individuals believe that Alyssa actually captured Aaron's aura on film. He was most likely lingering on earth for a few days after he died before he crossed into the light. Once again, if this were true, Aaron was proving beyond a doubt that he was not an ordinary son. To this day, all who view the pictures are astounded.

For me to state the above surprises me. I have moments where I think I am a player in a ghost story. Before my son died if someone had shown me pictures similar to Aaron's, I would not have believed them. I think people must say, "Mrs. Zabierek was such a nice lady, but then her son died and she hasn't been the same since." I always believed in ghosts. If there are ghosts, then where do the normal, good people go? If we are on this planet, then why can't there be more out there? So many things in this world are unexplainable. I then chose to believe there was more. My sanity depended on the belief that Aaron did not live in vain and he continued to live in another dimension. Sylvia Browne has become my mentor for the spiritual world. Her books explain the afterlife in a no-nonsense language. It's sort of "Afterlife for Dummies." Her books are inspirational to me, and she provides reasons for my belief in the signs and messages from my son.

The Emptiness Returns

Our vacation was over, and the rooms were complete. What was next? The emptiness was a heavy cloud that enveloped me. I had no aim or direction. My life before Aaron's death was very structured, organized and busy. I would maintain lists and plan every hour of every day. People would fault me for being so organized. I had nothing to plan. Every day was empty with no purpose. My only purpose was to think about my son and his death. I wanted answers. Did the afterlife exist? Was Aaron's life in vain? I had been raised as a Catholic. I had taken for granted the fact that Christ rose after death. Now I wanted to believe that he did rise from the dead. My purpose expanded into researching the afterlife. Alyssa and I visited the library. I took as many books as I could find. I spent my time reading and watching any programs I could find on television.

The books were fascinating. Every book had the same theme. The authors believed without a doubt that the afterlife existed. I connected to Sylvia Browne even more and read all of her books. Every question I had, she answered. It made sense to me. I needed to believe her. It is possible that prior to Aaron's death I may have shrugged off her books. This is not a topic that is freely discussed in society. I wish that I had read them while Aaron was alive. I do not think it would ease the pain of his death, but I would have been better prepared for the signs and acceptance of his death. My days were spent talking to Aaron and asking for signs. If I chose this path of belief, I wanted concrete proof. My husband jokes about this with me today. He imagines Aaron in heaven trying to explain to the other souls and God, "My mother is a doubting Thomas and you have to let me drop signs on her head!" I would receive a sign and be amazed. The next day I would begin to dissect the same sign. I would question whether it was a coincidence or a true sign. The following is a selection of signs we received.

I buried my rosary beads with Aaron. I read that the most important thing the living can do for the deceased is to pray for them. I wanted to say the rosary for Aaron, but I did not have any rosary beads to pray with. After a couple days of talking about the rosary beads, I received a package in the mail. My cousin had sent me rosary beads! The beads were also red!

The Band Director's Secretary, our very close friend, was cleaning out the band closet at the school. She emptied the closet and at the very back found an old trumpet case. As she pulled it out, she noticed that the case was covered in graffiti, written with white-out. She remembered Aaron's case and thought this could be his. Immediately she called me on the telephone. As she began to describe what had just happened, I stopped her as she was about to describe the case. I asked her if the case was covered in white writing. She stated excitedly that it was indeed covered in white writing. She brought the trumpet to my house that night. Gary and I were overjoyed. The trumpet was Aaron's. It was the original trumpet he had used when he began the school lessons in the fourth grade! He brought it to the high school to use during marching practice. He had a silver Bach trumpet, and we did not want him to use the expensive trumpet at practice. This trumpet sat at the high school for four years. My husband turned to me and said," You asked Aaron for a trumpet sign and he sent the most amazing sing. Are you happy?" I was indeed happy.

My husband and I were in the car. We were very quiet and both thinking about the accident. Driving in a car is one of the most difficult times. My husband turned on the radio to break up the deafening silence. The station was tuned in to one that he did not usually listen to, and a chorus of trumpets blared over the radio. We looked at each other and thought, Aaron is with us. About two minutes later we noticed in the median strip of the highway four deer! We wondered how the deer could have crossed the highway without getting hit by a car. My husband and I believe that a deer was in the road the day that Aaron had his accident. I turned to my husband and asked, "Is Aaron trying to tell us there was a deer in the road and he turned to avoid it?"

My cousin's daughter spent the night at my house. The following morning I asked the girls what they wanted for breakfast. They decided on bagels. I need to defrost them in the microwave. I took the bagels out of the freezer and walked to the microwave. In place of the time on the microwave, the word CHILD appeared. I was startled and yelled out. The girls came running into the kitchen. They saw the word as well. I then tried to clear the microwave. I could not. I began to get nervous and the girls said they were scared. I finally said out loud, "Okay, Aaron, please stop, you are scaring the girls." The microwave immediately cleared back to the correct time. I have never had that happen before. I took out the manual and searched for a reason. I could not find one. (I have read that spirits can affect electrical appliances very easily)

I wanted to accept the signs as confirmation that Aaron lived on. As I received each sign, I was encouraged and had a moment of hope. Soon after, some of the hope dissipated and I found myself saying if it is all true and I am willing to believe, why can't Aaron just appear to us? That would give me the confirmation I needed. As I awaited the end of summer, I spent my days reading and looking for answers.

Counseling

As I stated earlier, I wanted to be sure that nothing would happen to my family. I had already lost Aaron, and I could not bear to lose one of the girls or Gary. If something happened to Gary and me, the girls would be further devastated. This was the force that drove me. We agreed to continue to see a counselor. Although we had already seen a counselor, I did not feel that I had bonded with him. After speaking with my physician's office, I called another counselor. We had three sessions with this new counselor. The visits were very painful. We had to tell our story once again. Each time we told the story, we had to relive it. I could not complete a sentence without crying. Each session was very emotionally draining. I found that each session sent me into a downward spiral. I finally came to the realization that this man, whom we were confiding our deepest emotions to, did not know how we felt. He could assess us for medication, but he could not reassure us to the level that we needed. We did not feel a connection to him either.

Ironically, after our third session I received a message on the answer machine. Heidi left me a telephone number for a local Compassionate Friends Support Group. Her mother-in-law had attended a meeting and thought Gary and I could benefit from attending a session. Gary and I discussed the prospect of joining the support group. We decided to attend a meeting. After all, every parent in the room would know how we felt. We would finally be in a place where we belonged. This could be the connection for which I searched. The meetings were held the first Tuesday of every month. The next meeting would be the day after Labor Day, my first day returning to work and the girls' first day returning to school. What a day that would turn out to be.

Returning to Work

I did not want to return to work. I had built a safe cocoon around me at home. I felt safe and was afraid to leave. I ultimately returned to work for two reasons.

The first reason was for financial purposes. We could not afford to live without my paycheck. In order to keep my home, Aaron's home, I had to work. There is also the cost to bury a child. Parents never discuss this. We did have a small life insurance policy. However, we invested in that policy when Aaron was a baby. It did not cover the cost of the funeral. I am blessed to have family who offered some financial assistance. However, my son was nineteen years old and had his own set of bills. I love Aaron, but I do recognize his faults. He was not responsible with money. Some creditors were gracious, but others were not. We had co-signed on student loans and were still responsible for them. His car was not paid in full when it was totaled. He had the car five weeks, and the payoff did not cover the balance of the loan. I had no choice but to return to work.

The second reason was my girls. My daughters had to attend school. They did not have a choice because the state would not allow me to keep them home. They had to be in buildings, especially Ashley, where

Aaron had walked the corridors before them. These buildings held people who knew the Zabierek family and who knew Aaron. Someone could stop them in the hall and ask, "How was your summer?" There could be individuals who had been away for the summer and had not heard about Aaron's death. If my babies had to face this challenge, I could face my own challenge. After all, I worked for a small company. Every co-worker was familiar with my loss. I would not be surprised by the questions about my summer. This is the pool from which I drew my energy. My children gave me strength.

At Work

As I awoke on my first day to return to work, it was surreal to me. Preparing for work was a normal process, yet actually getting ready felt like the days before Aaron's death. It was almost as if the accident hadn't occurred. I had very real moments in which I thought the past two months were a dream. I would ask myself if it really had happened.

I entered the building. I felt that alone was an accomplishment. Every step of the way, I pondered turning back. I would think of the girls and continue on. Just to walk in the door was a task I thought I would never accomplish. I was very early. I wanted to avoid walking into people. One by one, they came to see me as they arrived. I am fortunate to work with amazing people. I was immediately surrounded with comfort, love, and caring people. Another safety net was formed around me.

I was able to tell my stories again. I had a captive audience that listened to my every word. They encouraged me to talk and describe my signs. Their reaction of amazement gave me more conviction to believe the signs. If many people agreed with my signs, then I was more confident in believing them myself. The old saying "The majority rules" sounded in my head. Don't be fooled, I had my moments. But, unlike when I was at home alone, when I had a lapse of utter sadness, I was immediately surrounded with concerned co-workers. I was never the type of person to handle tough times alone. I need people in my life. The word *loner* was not listed on my life's resume. At work, I was never alone. It turned out to be a better spot for me. I could dive into a project and actually forget for a moment. Soon the memories would come back like a deluge, but for five minutes I could have a rest. As the day progressed, the five minutes turned into ten minutes and so on.

Although life was returning to normal and I had let go of some of the negative feelings, a new problem occurred. Guilty feelings reared their ugly heads. I would stop in the middle of my day and be overcome with guilt, especially if I had laughed. How could I behave so normally when the most abnormal event had occurred in my life? How could I function when my son had died? Shouldn't I spend the rest of my life mourning him? I would think of my signs. If the signs were real, then Aaron lived on. He could see me. Aaron would be angry with me for behaving this way. I wanted to make my son proud. As any parent would agree, I did not want to cause my son worry. I tried to behave as a parent. I tried my best to not worry my extraordinary son.

The Meeting

I made it through the first day back. The girls also survived the first day of school. It was the countdown to survive. We'd cross off a day at a time. The time came for the Compassionate Friends Support Group meeting. As we drove to the meeting, the same anxious feeling emerged. What could we expect? We were the second couple to arrive. We completed paperwork and were ushered into the meeting room. The room was empty. My husband led us to the back of the room. I felt as if I were in school and did not want to sit in front of the teacher. As we approached the chairs he selected, I noticed they were covered in red fabric, Aaron's favorite color. As I sat in the chair, to my amazement, the pattern of the fabric consisted of dragonflies! This was a sign. I turned to Gary and said, "We are meant to be here." Next to us were two chairs that had been reserved with someone's purse. Ironically, Gary chose chairs next to the only two saved chairs. This would prove to be another sign. The couple that sat next to us had lost their son nine months before, also in a car accident. When we make a connection and meet real people who have suffered a loss similar to ours, it brings us some comfort. We are not alone. This happens to parents every day. They were still living and breathing, and that brought me comfort. It would ease some of the guilt I felt because I had attempted to go on without Aaron. If other parents could look normal and function normally, then I was not a bad parent for doing the same thing.

The meeting proved to be even more draining that the sessions with the counselor. So much pain in one small room. Every parent told his or her story. The devastation and sadness was almost too much to bear. When it was our turn, Gary could not talk, and I spoke. I was impressed by the sympathy in the eyes of the parents as I told our story. Sincere sympathy brings a small level of comfort. Gary and I did not have the strength to speak for the remainder of the meeting.

When the meeting concluded, we spoke with the couple that sat next to us, on the reserved seats. We gave each other details of our families and the situation of our sons' deaths. They assumed that we lived in Pelham, where Aaron died. Gary explained that we were from Methuen and lived near the Pelham town line. They were familiar with Methuen because of band activities with their son-in-law. We were astounded and explained Gary's involvement with the band. He was the Band Parents' Association President. They gave us their son-in-law's name. We were in shock. Their son-in-law was Aaron's trumpet tutor during his senior year of high school. I knew that instant that Aaron was sending us a sign. We were meant to attend that meeting. That couple had suffered the same loss that we did. Bad things happen to good people. We exchanged e-mail addresses and said our good-byes. As Gary and I drove home, we both were filled with such hope. That meeting gave us two strong signs. What are the odds that Aaron's trumpet tutor would lose his young brother-in-law and it would be followed by Aaron's death? If Gary had chosen another chair, we would not have talked to those parents. We were led to that spot. It was as if Aaron were saying, "Mom and Dad, you belong here and I am with you every step of the way."

A Friend

Just about every co-worker of mine had visited me at my home. One visit stood out more than the others did. A gentleman had just begun working with me during the past year. He came to see me. He had experience visiting with a mother who had lost her child. His very best friend had lost her daughter three years prior to Aaron's death. As he related the story, I realized that I had graduated from high school with his friend. I also had attended Brownies with her. Aaron also had attended high school with her daughter. Who would have thought that, as innocent children playing together, we would grow up to experience the same tragic event? He gave me her telephone number. He recommended that I call her. He told me it was deja vu listening to me. She said the same things as I did after she had lost her daughter. I wanted to call her. I needed a friend who could understand me. I did attempt to call her several times. Each time I did not finish dialing the number. This was a new face. I would have to relive my story. I finally completed the call. When I heard her voice, she brought me back to my childhood days. I was instantly comforted. She had survived three years without her daughter, and she sounded perfectly sane to me. We had a long conversation. She gave me some valuable information.

She first informed me of a memorial in my town square. I was unaware that this memorial was for children who had died in a tragic event. Their names were engraved in a marble bench that surrounded a lovely clock tower. Although I had seen the clock tower a thousand times, I never knew the true purpose of it. I wanted Aaron's name engraved on the bench. This comforted me. It was a way for me to keep him alive. With the help of my aunt, Aaron's name joined many other names on that bench. I'll explain my first visit to that memorial later.

The second piece of information that she gave me was just as valuable. I asked her how she survived. I wanted to know what she did to recover. She told me about a support group in town. The qualifications to join this group were simple. A mother had to have lost a child. I remember thinking there are enough of these mothers in my own town to form a group? My feeling of isolation started to dissipate. She gave me the details of the group meeting. She explained to me that she also needed to belong. She wanted to talk with another mother who had experienced the same tragedy that she had. These mothers did exist right next door. I promised myself that I would go to a meeting.

I also learned from her that her daughter was buried in the same cemetery as Aaron. I wanted to visit her daughter's grave. I did not have the courage to ask her where it was located. I called my coworker, hoping he could help me. He did not know where it was. His friend had moved to Florida and she did not visit her daughter's grave very often. My husband and I needed to visit Aaron's grave every Sunday. We began our search for her daughter's grave. I needed to visit it. I was slightly obsessed with finding that grave. I do not know why I needed to find that grave. I compare it to how a new mother seeks out other new mothers to compare babies. They compare the birth weight, length, sleeping patterns, and eating patterns. Did I want to compare graves the same way I compared him at birth? Did this give me the parenting I was missing? Although I was not having any luck, I still searched every week. As events occurred, I finally found her grave in the most amazing way. Details to follow, as I must describe other events as they occurred first.

A Visit to the Medium

Although the signs comforted me, I wanted more. I wanted to see John Edward. My cousin's wife made some inquiries for me, and to my disappointment the waiting list was very long and cost was too high. I did not have the patience to wait and could not rationalize spending so much money with other financial obligations as a result of Aaron's accident. I started to think that I did not need a famous medium. If Aaron was around me, he would definitely find a way to talk to me through whomever I chose. I prayed and asked for help. As others, in John's book, I asked for the other side to bring me to a medium. I believed I would receive a sign that would send me to a medium. I was testing the afterlife once again. I am such a "Doubting Thomas" that I usually drive my family crazy. To my surprise I received a sign. During one of the visits with my cousin's wife, she gave me the name of a medium with whom she had many sessions. She encouraged me to call the medium. I was not ready. That also was not a powerful enough sign for me!

About a week later I received a call from my husband's cousin. She called because she had received a sign from Aaron. Apparently Aaron's prayer card ended up in her bathroom, a most unlikely place. She had been thinking about Gary and me and then saw the card. She called me that same day. She talked of the time her brother died and her recovery from that loss. The reason for her call was to ask me if I had heard of John Edward. She encouraged me to visit a medium. She told me that I did not need a famous medium, but any medium. She gave me the name of a medium that she had visited often. She had amazing results with this medium and gave me the same name that my cousin's wife had given me! That was twice for the same medium, but as usual I look at the half-empty glass. I had another visit from my cousin's wife. This time she placed in my hand a business card for the medium. This was the third time. I finally got the message and scheduled the visit. I made an appointment for my husband and me. We would spend a half-hour together with this medium. The waiting began.

Making a Connection

The day had finally arrived. I could think of nothing else but that visit. Every moment I prayed to let Aaron speak to us. At times I would scream to Aaron in my mind. I begged him to talk to us. I was a bundle of nerves. My husband was having the same feelings as me. The drive was almost unbearable. I wanted to jump out of my skin. I have never been as anxious as I was that day. We arrived at her office. The waiting room was very calming. We waited for a few minutes. It seemed an eternity to us. We were called into the room. We sat down and the reading began immediately. I will list some excerpts below. Please keep in mind that I booked the appointment under my first name only. I gave no additional information and did not complete any paperwork. The visit was scheduled only two weeks prior and was a minimal fee of $40.00.

> _The medium –" Immediately I am going to come to your energy (Gary) and say that, God, it feels like you have had the rug pulled right out from under you. Can you understand that when I say that to you? Sometimes we feel like we're going_

through a grieving process and it feels to me like you've placed a wall of protection around you from the grieving also. It says I don't want to feel this. This feels too painful to me. I'm going to go inside. I'm going to close the door and I'm not going to let anybody in, 'cause I don't want to trust life any more. And I feel like that's going to be very hurtful to you, and we have to come back out and play. Have we lost a child? 'Cause I feel we have. Big time. But that child needs you to know that they don't want to be held responsible for you not living your life anymore."

"I truly feel that every soul has an idea as to how long it's going to stay here. And I feel that your child knew it wasn't going to stay to become an old person. Do you understand that? Whether they shared this information with you at some time in their life, that I know I am not going to be an old person. I feel that you have to remember what this child was trying to say to you. So that you can understand the soul knew...the soul of that child knew."

"There are other people in this lifetime that you need to be supportive to. Do we have three children? Because I feel you are the parents of three children. So what the soul of the one that left is trying to say is that there are two others. All right? You need to be understanding of and you can't shut them out because of what happened."

"Was this a son? 'Cause I feel it was. He's saying a son."

"He's telling me he left quickly. Do you understand that? And so there's this feeling that I want you to know I was in no pain. All right? I want you to know I left so quickly that there was no pain at all. All right? Because I feel that you (Deb) question this. I was pulled out so quickly that I didn't feel pain. He wants you to know that he was unsure as to how it happened because it happened so quickly. I went to sleep right away. It's sort of like I went to sleep right away."

"Now has your dad passed over? (Gary) So he's talking about a grandfather to you on your dad's side of the family and that he has met the Father."

"Was there a car issue here? Yes, because he's showing me this car as if there was a car issue here. And I feel confused about the car. So whether we are confused as to how it all happened. All right. I feel as if we don't know the particulars as far as this incident is concerned and he's saying he doesn't either, because it happened so quickly, but I don't feel he was at fault. Can you understand that? I didn't intentionally drive a car and not have any responsibility behind driving the car. All right? I don't feel that he was at fault. And there's this I need you to know that I wasn't reckless, all right, as far as this situation

is concerned. That I didn't intentionally drive a car and not have any responsibility behind driving the car. He wants you to know that he wasn't the cause of this but that he is unsure as to how it all happened because it happened so quickly. To him, I went to sleep right away. It's sort of like I went to sleep right away."

"Was he still in school? Was he heading toward schooling? 'Cause I feel like I am moving toward a training, a schooling of some kind. (Gary explains that Aaron left Norwich) So I need you to know I would have gone back. All right? I feel that this would have made you happy as hell if I had said this to you and I'm sorry that I didn't say this to you."

"I feel that you've been seeing him in dreams. Do you understand that? And I feel that it's his way of letting you know he is there."

"In and out of girlfriend issue. And that this was a big issue. I don't want people to feel because I was that way I got behind the wheel and here again didn't demonstrate my responsibility because that was the last thing on my mind as I was in the car."

"Who's John? We have a grandfather here? I feel like it's a grandfather. (I explain that I have a grandfather John.) Yes. Has your grandfather passed over? He walks with John, that grandfather, is what he is saying. So even

though he might not have remembered him well or knew him well he just needs you to know I knew who he was because he told me who he was."

"Why is the car red? He's validating the color red to you."

"Where does the K come from? They walk together. It feels like a boys' team on the other side of life. They have something in common, middle name and this man's name and that they walk together too. He left rather quickly too. They didn't suffer."

"I feel that he is gong to keep on coming to you in dreams. I feel that you could have a nap in the afternoon and he could show up. So don't limit yourself to how he could show up to you. I feel that he came in the car with you."

We left that session speechless. Our immediate impression was comfort. We both felt a sense of peace wash over our senses. Momentarily the pain was subdued. I can only compare it to how one feels after a long cry. The body is drained and almost lethargic. However, shortly into the drive home, the questions began. Was Aaron really in the room? How could she know that stuff if he wasn't? She had said some additional personal information to us, and we were blown away by the factual details. Amazement was prevalent in our emotions. We wanted to call everyone and relay the session. I believe that was the moment when my faith in the afterlife began to deepen. Aaron did exist and had been with us every day since his death. How else could this stranger know our personal life? She talked about how his soul knew that he would not live to be an old person. He made that pact with Emily about placing roses in the casket. Why would a young person speak of dying unless he had a sense of it deep within his soul? Aaron did tell friends that he would not live to be an old person. We were informed of this only after Aaron died. These friends had no idea that we went to the medium. He also brought one of his best friends to a cemetery on several occasions. He even selected a song to be played at his funeral, unbeknownst to my husband and me. Was this a coincidence?

She spoke at length about the accident. She described the accident. Critics could say that she gathered her information from the newspapers, but she pinpointed my concerns about Aaron causing the accident. The papers did not convey that this was a concern of mine. I began to ask these questions immediately after he died. I also questioned whether the girlfriend issue had depressed him. The medium was accurate. My questions were answered and my extraordinary son was comforting me.

As she spoke about Aaron meeting the father, Gary and I were both curious about the words, "the father." Why didn't he say, "I met my grandfather or great-grandfather? " We remembered my mother-in-law's sign and believed that Aaron was trying to tell us that he met our Pastor. Aaron was very involved in the church around the time of the Pastor's death. A connection was made, and we believe that Aaron was using this term to validate to us that he was indeed in heaven.

Gary and I dissected the entire reading. She provided names of loved ones. The facts spoke for themselves. At that moment we both believed that Aaron lived on and was still with us every day. This reading also bridged that gap between what the books described and my former opinion on the afterlife, especially the theory regarding the planning of one's life. I had some knowledge and this gave me the power to continue. This power was the life-nurturing water for the seeds of my soul.

His Birthday

Alyssa and Aaron shared the month of October for their birthdays. Aaron was born two weeks past his due date of October 7, 1982. Alyssa was born two weeks prior to her due date of October 21, 1988. Each of them was born on the other's due date. Alyssa's birthday was arriving, yet I could only focus on Aaron's birthday. I could hold her and kiss her on her birthday, but I could not hold or kiss Aaron. Being a child, she was excited for her birthday to arrive. I forced myself to be positive and focus on Alyssa. I gathered strength from her joy.

Customarily we celebrated birthdays by hosting a family party on the weekend. The actual birthday was celebrated with a special dinner at the restaurant of the child's choosing. Alyssa began to talk about the restaurant she would be choosing for her birthday dinner. Gary and I both agreed that it would be difficult to leave Ashley home alone while we took Alyssa out to dinner. We decided to change the tradition and have Ashley join the three of us for the dinner celebration. At first, Alyssa was disappointed that she had to share her night, but we explained our reason and she welcomed Ashley.

As usual Alyssa gave us a list of gift suggestions. At the top of her list was a cell phone. Prior to Aaron's death, this was out of the question. We discussed cell phones with Alyssa and explained to her that she had to wait until she was sixteen years old, like her brother and sister. She was not a happy camper. Things changed, and Gary and I simultaneously decided that Alyssa should have a cell phone. Our reasons were purely selfish. As parents who had lost a child, we needed to know the whereabouts of our surviving children. When Alyssa opened her gift, she was delighted. Whatever our reason was, she was happy. Someone at the party commented that she was young to own a cell phone. Didn't they realize why I needed her to have a cell phone?

As the fall settled in, this roller coaster ride was never ending. From one day to the next, we did not know if we were climbing the hill or flying down the other side of the hill. One thought that definitely put us at the bottom of the hill was the approach of Aaron's birthday. October 21st was around the corner. Instead of celebrating his 20th birthday, his absence would be magnified on the anniversary of the first day he entered our lives. How could we possibly survive that day? What would we do for the twenty-four hours it took for the day to pass? Father David offered to preside over a memorial mass for Aaron's birthday. I believed I could not enter the church again so soon. He suggested that we have the mass in our home. Gary and I liked that idea. We decided to have the birthday mass for Aaron on October 20, 2002 in our home.

The scheduling of the mass gave us a distraction. We began to plan. My husband is an incredible man. His dedication and love for his son shone at this time. Gary is typically very particular when organizing a function. His skills have been enhanced over time through his work. He has a reputation for hosting elegant functions. We made lists and organized the mass. Gary thought of everything, down to the music. He made plans to rearrange the living room furniture. His goal was to turn our living space into a chapel. I planned the menu. Ashley's friends heard of the mass and offered their services. The well of support from family and friends was still flowing. Every detail was taken care of.

Aaron's stone was due to arrive days before his birthday. Father David suggested that we drive to the cemetery at the conclusion of the mass. Upon arriving at the cemetery, he would say a prayer and bless the stone. Since several of our family members lived out of town, this would give them all an opportunity to view the stone. It was important for Gary and me to have our friends and family view Aaron's memorial. We began to look forward to the day of the mass. It was evolving into a special day to honor Aaron.

The Memorial

Just prior to the memorial mass, Gary received a call from the Monument Company. Aaron's head stone was completed and had been placed at the cemetery. Gary and I both agreed that we wanted to view the stone for the first time as a family. I left work and we timed it for them to leave home so we would arrive at the same time. I was anxious as I drove. My stomach felt host to an unwelcome soccer game. I pulled into the cemetery and turned onto Aaron's street. As I inched down the street, I could see the stone! Although I had the tree as a landmark, the new addition gleamed in the sunlight. I was filled with excitement. Gary had arrived just before me, but they waited to get out of the car. My car came to a stop, and now I could see the stone clearly. The name Zabierek gleamed in the sunlight. The stone stood out like a beacon. We anxiously approached the stone. The black marble was magnificent, and the engraving was a masterpiece. The detail was exquisite, right down to the four sparkling stars. This memorial did tell a story about my son. If a stranger walked past this stone, he would know that my son played the trumpet. He would contemplate the mountain scene and most likely believe this was a significant part of Aaron's life. The story on the front of the stone would naturally lead him to walk around the back. There he would see two of Aaron's loves in life, soccer and hockey. My husband and I had fulfilled our goal. Not only was this stone a beacon in a gray sea, it portrayed a story about Aaron.

As we stood in front of this memorial, the feelings are indescribable. We all reacted emotionally. Although the stone was magnificent and we were pleased with it, this stone sealed the deal, so to speak. This was the final chapter of burying my son. If I did not believe that he was gone before, now it was before me in writing. Another chapter in our lives, without Aaron, was closed.

The Mass

I awoke the morning of the Mass. It was a solemn yet positive day. Forty-five guests were coming to our home to attend the Mass. I would never have anticipated hosting a Mass in my home. Was this my extraordinary son at work behind the scene? My husband and I were fulfilling our parental duties and having a birthday celebration for Aaron. Aaron was gone and could no longer have parties from Mom and Dad, yet this was an avenue for us to be parents again. This enabled us to be positive while we planned the event, but the reality was that we were having this Mass in place of a birthday party. Mixed emotions swirled inside each of us, while happy emotions battled sad emotions.

My husband is a master at planning parties and this was no exception. He transformed our home into a chapel. Chairs were lined up parallel to each other to replicate pews. He created an altar from my dining room table and a white linen cloth. Aaron's graduation picture was placed on an easel next to the altar. Gary even thought of religious music. He had taken me to a shop which sold religious items. There was a display of tapes containing religious music. We listened to every tape until he selected the perfect one. He then spoke to my cousin and set up our stereo with a remote so that he could play Gary's choices on cue. The chapel was complete and we stood to admire his creation. The doorbell rang at that exact moment. A bouquet of a dozen red roses greeted me when I opened the door! The one missing item was an arrangement of flowers in front of the altar. My girlfriend, from work, sent me this amazing bouquet. Without realizing it, she had completed the chapel.

The guests began to arrive. As each one entered my home the sadness in their eyes changed to amazement when they saw the chapel. One special guest arrived with a surprise for us. My cousin's husband had crafted a display case for Aaron's trumpet. We knew that he was creating this for us but did not expect it to be ready on this day. As he walked through my front door with this magnificent case in his arms, I was no longer able to suppress the tears. Emotions took over and the broken dam released a flood of tears.

Father David was the last to arrive. He was impressed with Gary's chapel. He prepared to serve the Mass. I have to admit it was a wondrous feeling to have a priest in my home preparing for Mass. In my wildest dreams I could not have imagined this. My daughters each read a selection from the Bible. The music played on cue. Communion was served to all. Father David honored Aaron and touched every soul in that little chapel. My son was extraordinary to leave such a legacy deserving of this.

Completing this tribute to Aaron was the blessing of Aaron's stone by Father David. We planned to have all of our guests join us in a procession to the cemetery. At the conclusion of the Mass, we all entered our cars. In a small motorcade we processed to the cemetery. Most of the group would be viewing the stone for the first time. Their reactions were as expected. Everyone was amazed. At that moment Gary and I were proud parents. At least on this day we were able to be the parents to Aaron that we longed to be. Father David blessed the stone. Ashley read one of her poems. The very special birthday celebration for our son was complete.

We invited everyone back to our home, to share a meal. I had recruited some of my daughter's friends to disassemble the chapel and set up for a buffet. I actually demonstrated how I wanted to arrange the table and the food. I provided written instructions and pictures. They laughed at me. But when we returned home, the house looked great. My daughter's friends confessed that they could not have done it without my drawings and instructions! I like to think that they also had help from above. Gary and I enjoyed a good meal with family and friends. We ate, talked, and reminisced about Aaron. There were even some laughs as we all told Aaron stories. It proved to be a very special, wonderful memorial to our extraordinary son.

Wal-Mart

I took many pictures of the stone as well as Gary's temporary chapel. Since Gary's sister was in California, she could not go to the cemetery. She was anxious to see Aaron's memorial stone. Through the lens we could share our experience with the Mass and memorial.

I brought the film to work and it was my intention to drop it off at Wal-mart when I got out of work. I was not feeling well at the end of the day. I decided to skip the picture run and I went directly home. At some point I changed my mind. After all, I still had to take Alyssa to dance so I redirected myself and dropped the film off at the one-hour photo shop at Wal-Mart. I then picked Alyssa up for dance. I drove back to Wal-Mart. As I walked to the back of the store, a woman caught my eye. She was walking slowly looking at pictures. She was headed in the same direction as me. I arrived at the photo department counter. She walked up beside me. As I gave my name, she stated that she had the wrong pictures. While the clerk searched for my pictures, I glanced in the woman's direction. I looked at her pictures and recognized Aaron's picture from the chapel. I said, "Those are my pictures." She then said to me that she knew they weren't hers because she had taken pictures of her husband's stone and the stone in the picture was not his stone. I said I also had taken pictures of a stone and that the stone was my son's. She gave me the photos and the clerk found her photos. We both had film developed of our loved one's memorial stones! She asked where Aaron was buried and I told her. Her husband was also in the same cemetery! She also asked me how Aaron died. For the first time in public I told his story. She remembered the article in the paper as well as a few strangers nearby, who were enthralled with us. We shared our photos and stories. She especially wanted me to see the flower arrangement on her husband's stone. She had a saddle arrangement made for the top of his stone and that is why she photographed it. We gave each other the locations of the stones. She made a promise to me that she would stop by Aaron's stone and pray for him. She was an angel to me. I walked out of the store that day in a fog. I don't recall the drive home. Our names were not even close in the alphabet. How did our photos get switched? I did not even want to go to the store that day. If I have not arrived at that exact moment, I would not have seen her. Was it fate? Did destiny bring us together? Were Aaron and her husband together on the other side?

This amazing story continues. The following Sunday we went to the cemetery. After we visited Aaron's grave, I wanted to find this woman's husband's grave. Based on her directions, we drove to find the stone. The stone was easily spotted because of the arrangement on top of it. We parked the car and walked to the stone. I paused at the stone and prayed for him. I also asked him to say hello to my son. Sometimes I think I am losing my mind. As I turned to leave, something caught my attention at the neighboring stone. I waked to this stone. I knelt in front of the stone to see it closely. As I read the stone, I realized this was the stone of my childhood friend's daughter! I was absolutely amazed. I called for my husband. I was so excited and spoke so quickly he did not understand me at first. Once I calmed down, he understood what I was telling him. His eyes reflected my wonder as well. He was just as amazed as I was. I found her stone! My search ended! She was buried next to this Wal-Mart gentleman. Divine intervention must have been at work. Too many events, especially the picture mix up, occurred to bring me to this spot. If I had not gone into Wal-Mart at that exact moment, I would not have met the woman. Why did our pictures get mixed up? Our last names were not even remotely close in the alphabet. The moment that I realized that the Wal-Mart visit was the connection to this stone, a blanket of hope enveloped me. This couldn't be a coincidence! My mission in life was to find concrete proof of the afterlife. Was this not evidence in my case? Once I proved that the afterlife existed, I would have peace because Aaron lived on. I convinced myself that Aaron had sent me to Wal-Mart that day. He had answered a prayer of mine. He existed and could hear me! I loved my extraordinary son more than I could have ever imagined.

Another Support Group

As the days dragged on, the monotony of life could be soothing as well as maddening. Every moment of every day was filled with thoughts of Aaron. I tried to make sense of the accident and accept that it happened. I could not understand it. Aaron was gone and I was still shocked that this had happened to my family. How could I ever get past this dark time? I was searching for medicine to cure this ailment. Did any exist? I had to admit that, although my coping mechanisms had improved since the summer, I was far from being completely recovered. Was that even possible? A friend had given me information about another support group. This group was comprised of local mothers who had lost a child. I did not know that such a group existed. It also surprised me that there were enough women in my town who had lost a child to form a group. I decided to attend this group. I was still searching for a friend who had experienced the same tragedy as I did. Maybe she existed and would be at this group.

    I had to attend this meeting alone and that was a challenge for me. As I pulled into the parking lot, I summoned all of my strength to stop myself from driving immediately to the exit sign. I did not want to do this again. Another mother spotted me and brought me into the meeting. It was a small meeting. Many members were not present. My first reaction was a positive one. The group was not overwhelming. The women were compassionate. I believed that I belonged to this group. I found a home. The meeting started and each woman shared her experience with the group. This is a morbidly difficult task. I wanted to skip this part. I still was unable to get the story out without succumbing to tears. When the last mother had shared her story, the conversation took an interesting turn. The subject of mediums and spirits was introduced. This was my forum. I loved talking about this topic. I summoned my strength and began to retell my experience with the medium. I held a captive audience. As I looked into their eyes, I could see hope seeping in. They had questions and were encouraged with my words. I talked for two hours. Anybody who knows me will tell you that I love to talk. This meeting provided me with an outlet to alleviate some darkness. The mothers wanted the name of my medium. They believed in the afterlife. One mother talked about how she would not wish her son to be back on earth. She stated that heaven was such a wonderful place filled with love. Why would she wish for him to return to a place filled with pain and suffering? She gave me something to think about. If I believed in heaven, I had to agree with her. As I drove home, I sobbed. Tears cleanse the soul. Not only was my soul cleansed, but I had a dose of the medicine I was desperately searching for.

My Youngest Child

While my healing continued, the focus of most days for me was my children. If I was not consumed with thoughts of Aaron, my other children were on my mind. I wondered daily if they were really doing as well as they seemed. Did they have hidden pain that was slowly eating away at their souls? Often times a parent misses signs of trouble with her child. I worried that one day I would face another challenge with one of my daughters. My fear was that they would experience a breakdown or some form of addiction. I attempted to have a conversation with them. I desperately wanted them to confide in me. At times they would talk, but I never really believed they were sharing their true feelings. This is typical of teenagers, but I could not accept it.

One day while driving in the car with Alyssa, I was lucky to share in a deep, emotional conversation with her. We were driving past the church, which happens to be next to the funeral parlor where we had Aaron's services. As we were driving past the church, Alyssa said, "I don't want to go to CCD any more." I asked why. She would not give me details. She just continued to state that she did not want to attend the classes. She wasn't even sure if she wanted to be part of the Catholic religion. I persisted and she finally confessed the root of her worry. At the last CCD class her teacher had discussed heaven and her opinion of what was required to gain access to heaven. She actually told my daughter that if a person were to steal or lie he/she would not go to heaven. Being the sister of Aaron, Alyssa panicked. She loved Aaron but is old enough to know that he was not a saint. This teacher convinced her that there was a possibility that Aaron would not be in heaven. This was especially true because he had not attended church or confession prior to his death.

I explained to her that Gary and I had made the decision to raise our children as Catholics and we had completed this task with Aaron and Ashley. I had no intention of changing our religion with Alyssa. She would complete the program just as her brother and sister had completed it. She did not want to accept this. She was very upset and extremely emotional. My heart ached for her. I found myself telling her the real reason why I would not let her quit or have our family change religions. Aaron was a Eucharist Minister with the Catholic church. Father David was Aaron's friend and a Catholic priest. He was the reason that we had a personal and touching funeral for Aaron. He performed a mass in my home. Father David and the Catholic religion were my connection to Aaron. I could never leave this religion or church. I don't think I realized this until I actually spoke the words. I had to remain a Catholic and stay connected to Father David for Aaron. Aaron died as a Catholic. I buried Aaron as a Catholic. I would remain a Catholic until I was reunited with Aaron. She seemed to understand my reasoning although she was still upset.

I gave her permission to speak directly to the teacher the next time this topic was discussed in class. I advised her to raise her hand and directly ask the teacher, "My brother was only nineteen years old and was killed in a car accident. Because he did not go to confession, is he in hell?" She accepted that and it seemed to empower her. This child of mine is very mature for her age. She is very confident and not afraid to speak her mind. I believed that if this incident arose again, she would most definitely have the courage to ask such a question. I continued to comfort her. I also explained that although we are Catholic, we do not have to follow every rule. I believe that God is not just Catholic, and heaven is not only for the Catholic religion. God exists and is about faith. Each religion is a vehicle to practice faith and believe in God. Alyssa and I bonded and I was grateful.

<u>The Hypnotist</u>

Fall was settling in. This is my favorite time of the year. I love the smell of fall. It's a spicy smell that tickles my nose. Glossy red apples with bright orange pumpkins warm my heart. The air is crisp and the trees are giant bouquets of colorful leaves. The arrival of fall also previews the biggest holidays of the year. These would be our first holidays of importance, without Aaron. My favorite season, the prelude to the joyful times, was now tainted. I had this feeling of impending doom. A war was about to start, and I had no armor to defend myself. I needed to do something to prepare myself.

Every author, of books that I read, spoke about the fact that nothing on earth was an accident. Our life on earth is carefully planned. Nothing happens by chance. They also spoke about reincarnation. My childhood memories of reincarnation are different from what they were stating. I thought that one died and then chose to come back to earth in a different body. I imagined souls in heaven peeking down and looking for the special body to jump into. The psychics and mediums spoke of a very different reincarnation. Reincarnation, as I understand it now, is the soul choosing to come back to earth in a different life. This life is carefully planned years ahead. I now imagine a soul in heaven poring over a manuscript. This manuscript is filled with lessons and experiences that a soul desires. Family members choose to come back to earth together. All family members and special friends are souls that have traveled together many times. Therefore, I planned this life and came to earth knowing that Aaron would die at the age of nineteen. This was tough to swallow. My husband especially does not buy this theory. He asks me, "Why would I come to earth and choose this pain?" I find myself saying, "Maybe you never experienced loss before, or maybe Aaron experienced loss with you and now he is returning the favor." Was I crazy? Some of the mediums, in the books, actually hypnotize a person to travel back in time to a previous life. In one of the books a mom whose teenage son was hit by a car and killed was hypnotized. She traveled to the previous life that she had shared with her son. This experience helped her to understand why she came to earth knowing she would lose him. I wanted to experience this. I thought that if I could learn of a past relationship with Aaron, it would help me understand why he had left so early this time.

Ironically, my husband worked with a woman who had been hypnotized for a similar reason. His co-worker was successful, so I decided to visit the hypnotist. The appointment was on Saturday so that Gary could drive me. I was extremely anxious and nervous. The day did not start out on a good note. We had difficulty finding the office. As a result, we were late. After a half-hour of driving around and attempting to call the hypnotist, we finally found the office. Needless to say, I was highly emotional. This is not the state of mind to be in when visiting a hypnotist. She was very kind and relaxing, but I could not go under. As her soothing voice guided me to sleep, I could not clear my mind. As I lay on her couch, I would think that my nose was itchy. I would think of meeting Aaron and having a two-way conversation. My expectations were high and I was not relaxed. These ingredients stopped me from traveling to my past. I was devastated. She suggested that I use relaxation tapes and practice relaxing and clearing my mind. She believed that, if I did this, the hypnotism might work the next time. I rescheduled the visit and promised myself that I would try the tapes.

I bought a relaxation tape and listened to it. I learned that the key to a successful hypnotism is an empty mind. I had to learn to clear my mind from all thoughts. I believed that I learned as much as I could and was ready for another session. The second time, she scheduled me for a session in her home. She believed that I would relax easier in her home. I drove myself this time. I wanted to appear confident. I did arrive at her house in a completely different frame of mind from the last visit with her. She was kind and soothing. She did a relaxation technique with me prior to the session. I did relax much more easily this time, but I am not sure that I was hypnotized. I never actually saw Aaron in my mind, nor did I visit a past life. As she asked me questions, my response was "no" to each of them. She then instructed me to say the first thing that came into my mind. She was basically trying to construct a story. I was not an easy subject. I wanted to see Aaron and talk to him. I did give some information that led her to believe I was alive in the pioneer days. I may have been abused. When she changed direction and asked for help from Jesus and Mary so that I could have a visit with Aaron, I spoke about the ocean. I almost had a vision of visiting Aaron at the ocean with my grandfather. I did not have a conversation with him. I also did not see him clearly. It was vague and not what I expected. I tend to have very high expectations. A trait that gives me troubles. I was surprised to learn that I was with her for one hour. It seemed like twenty minutes to me. Did I visit Aaron? Although I did not get answers, I am proud of myself for trying. Maybe some day I will try again.

Additional Support

I received a telephone call from a member of the mothers' support group. Another meeting was scheduled and she invited me to attend. I decided that, with the impending holidays, a visit to the meeting was in order. Everything I read on the topic of surviving the loss of a child referred to the first event without the child as the most challenging, specifically the holidays. Christmas in the Zabierek household is an absolute favorite. We have many traditions, and the house is decorated from top to bottom. I tried to imagine this favorite time of year without Aaron, and my heart would almost stop. It was going to be impossible to get through the first Christmas without him. If I attended this meeting, maybe the mothers would offer their suggestions on how they survived the holidays.

I arrived early. I am a prompt person and hate to be the last to arrive. I settled in the corner, and before long the room filled. There were more mothers at this meeting than the last. The meeting started with each mother telling her story. This is such a difficult task. Most could not finish their story without tears. Try to imagine sitting in a room and hearing stories like mine over and over again. A blanket of sadness draped the entire room. This dark blanket was suffocating me.

I had all I could do not to run out of the room. I did not want to belong to this group. However the harsh reality was that I did belong. I had a tragic story just like every other mother in the room. So I stayed and listened while I waited for my turn. I barely managed to tell my story. I forced myself to finish so that we could continue with the meeting. I sat back and looked forward to their advice.

The advice never came. The meeting continued to spiral downward into further darkness. The mothers compared medication. Each talked about the kind she was on and how long she had been taking it. They talked about the therapy sessions. They talked about the reluctance to return to work. This was not me. I was already back at work. I was not on medication. These mothers had lost their children years before me, yet they were in the same dark place that I was in. Some were in darker places. This was not what I had bargained for. I wanted to talk about the holidays. I wanted to run from that room. I was afraid that if I ran I would continue to run and not stop. I sat frozen in my chair watching the clock.

Finally, a mother spoke about Christmas. I sat up and listened. She served a devastating blow. She was not going to celebrate Christmas again that year. She hadn't celebrated since the death of her daughter four years prior. I could not comprehend this. What about the surviving members of the family? I could not tell my girls that we would never celebrate Christmas. They deserved the same childhood that Aaron had been given. That childhood included Christmas. This was not an option for me. I moved to leave. Another mother mentioned Thanksgiving. I sat back down again. I was reaching for hope. I wanted advice. This might be it. She was going to set a place for her son at the table. I could not imagine anything more horrible than an empty chair waiting for Aaron. I left the meeting.

I sat in my car and cried. These mothers were not better than I was. I could not imagine feeling so empty and sad for years. I drove out of the parking lot and headed home. Luckily I came to a red light as I turned on the main street. I sat at the light and tried to gather my strength. I needed to drive home and face my family. If they had a good day, I did not want to drag them down. Then something caught my eye. The light that my car was stopped at faced the clock tower. The clock tower was a memorial for children in the town. Ironically, the mothers in the group were a part of the group that had established the memorial. Through the aid of my aunt, Aaron's name was going to be added to the memorial bench. I decided to pull over and walk to the memorial. Maybe Aaron's name had already been etched. I got out of my car and summoned strength to walk over to the memorial. As I approached the bench, Aaron's name stood out like a beacon. It had been etched! I sat down and let my fingers trace every letter in his name. I was so happy to see his name carved in the stone. His life would be remembered forever. I imagined a day when the town was unrecognizable, yet the bench that stood on that spot would display Aaron's name. I was comforted by this. I did not want to think that his short life was in vain. I am grateful to my aunt for being the catalyst to this meaningful tribute. I breathed a sigh of relief. I thanked the mothers. If I had not attended that meeting, I would have never seen his name. Did my extraordinary son lead me to it?

I Don't Belong

When I arrived at work the next morning, I was depressed and spiraling down very fast. It was one of those mornings that I was desperately trying to hang on. It took all of my strength just to sit in my chair and hold my head up straight. A group of co-workers were having a conversation. I wandered out of my office to join in. I am an extremely curious person. They were talking about their children. This was a conversation that happened frequently in an office of many women. On this particular day I could not join in. This was the straw that broke the camel's back, so to speak. My emotions let go. I did not belong. I had not fit in at the meeting last night, and now I did not fit in at work. I felt completely isolated from the world. Naturally my co-workers attempted to comfort me. I shared the story of my meeting the night before. I told them that I did not belong at the meeting and now I believed that I did not belong at work. I described my feeling of isolation. At that moment I believed I was completely alone. I was standing on a deserted island by myself with no hopes of rescue. One woman turned to me and said, "Debbie, you are not alone. Although we have not lost a son, we have shared this with you. We love you. You belong to us. You are the same person that you were before Aaron died and we still love you.

Let us be there for you." They all agreed with her. They told me that through my stories they experienced some of my emotions. They were eager to travel this road with me and remain at my side.

This moment was a turning point for me. I had been searching for someone just like me. I believed that because of my tragedy I needed to find a new life with new friends. I thought that my friends had to have experienced the same loss. I suddenly realized that I was wrong. Instead of searching for new friends, I could keep my old friends. Instead of creating a new life after losing Aaron, I could continue to live my old life, but without him.

The Long and Winding Road

So, I pulled up my bootstraps and headed back out on the long and winding road. Although there were mountains up ahead of me, I decided to continue on this path. I was committed to facing every hill and mountain in front of me, no matter the size. I truly believed that I did not have a choice. My surviving children came first and I vowed to trudge on for their sake.

I have stated many times before that it is the support and love of the people around me that provide me with the strength to get out of bed every day. This is an understatement. I am truly blessed. A scholarship fund was started for Aaron. His former band director presented us with a very special memorial for Aaron. He established a scholarship in Aaron's name. This scholarship would be given to a graduating band senior who exemplified the qualities of Aaron. The scholarship was offered for the next four years. Gary and I vowed to continue with this scholarship for as long as possible after the initial four years.

We set up the scholarship with a local bank. Two very special women took the initiative to organize a fundraiser for the scholarship. One was my aunt and the other was the mother of Aaron's best friend. Both women worked in the school system. Employees were offered the opportunity to wear blue jeans on a Friday for one dollar. Each dollar collected would be donated to Aaron's scholarship. The fundraiser was done at the school where each worked. Both events were extremely successful. These fundraisers emotionally moved Gary and me. I don't believe that these women realized the impact of what they had done. Gary and I were so grateful and comforted by their kindness and the generosity of all involved. This was the medicine that I needed. I believed that if people were going to show their support in such a grand way, then I could get out of bed every day. Their kindness was transformed into strength for me. Aaron's memory would be preserved in the high school for many, many years. What more could a mother ask for her extraordinary son?

Reminders

Another difficult task is watching one of my daughters do something that Aaron did. With only one son and two daughters, there were not many events that the girls would repeat. However, Ashley was approaching a time in her life that would mimic Aaron's last two years with us. Ashley was graduating from high school and would be beginning the process of choosing a college. Ironically, the fall after Aaron died would be the start of Ashley's college search. The memories of Aaron's college search were very fresh in our minds. The first college open house was to a local state college. I invited my Godchild Heather on the tour. She is Alyssa's age and I thought she would enjoy seeing a college. I also thought having the three girls would be a welcome distraction.

I awoke to the pitter-patter of rain. The day was dark and dreary. Where was the sunshine? The weather alone was depressing. Did I need this atmosphere to add to my day? I truly believe that if I did not have bad luck, I would have no luck at all. Nevertheless, I had to be optimistic for the gang. Contrary to my mood, everyone appeared to be in good spirits that morning. I decided not to express my concerns to Gary or the girls. The trip commenced. The girls were a welcome distraction. The incessant chatter helped to quiet my mind. I couldn't have dwelled on the pain if I wanted to, with the noise bubbling out from the back seat! It was a good decision to bring Heather.

We arrived at the school. As I got out of the car, my stomach lurched. My mind did a fast rewind, just like a videotape. After a blur of colors in my mind, I pictured myself getting out of the car at Norwich University, with Aaron beside me. But as I turned my head, Aaron was not beside me; it was Ashley. I fought back the tears. I had to be brave for Ashley. This was her day, not Aaron's day.

Heather's pants were too long and were quickly absorbing what seemed like every rain drop. As the wet line quickly seeped up her pant leg, the girls giggled. I was distracted once again by life.

We entered the lobby. Immediately we were welcomed by the familiar sounds of a trumpet. Ashley stopped in her tracks, and we all stopped right behind her. She simply turned to me and said, "Aaron is with me." It was music to my ears. A group of Jazz Band students were rehearsing for the open house. The sound of a trumpet makes my heart smile. What a coincidence that this trumpet player was rehearsing at the exact moment that we entered the room. It wasn't a coincidence because Aaron was beside me after all. My son is extraordinary.

Thanksgiving

I opened my eyes on Thanksgiving morning. I lay in my bed waiting for something to happen. The other shoe did not drop. I said to myself, "Deb, get out of bed and put that bird in the oven." I sat up and put my feet on the floor. I began the preparations for the dinner, while I waited for the other shoe to drop. As each family member awoke, there was the unspoken dread between us. Each was waiting for the other to cry or something.

We had decided to visit Aaron's grave in the morning. When the girls awoke, we got in the car and headed to the cemetery. We wanted to be together as a family and light Aaron's candle. Whenever we are all together at the cemetery, it gets very emotional for us. Yet when Gary and I go alone, we do not cry every time. I think when the four of us are there together, the empty space for Aaron is most noticeable. Gary lit the candle and we all kissed the stone. We all stood quietly. I wondered what each of them was thinking. Were they talking to Aaron? Were they praying? I guess they do what I do. Sometimes I pray, sometimes I ask questions, and sometimes I think nothing. After a few minutes, the silence was deafening. We started to leave. I said aloud, "Aaron, we need to know that you are with us on this holiday, so send us a big sign."

We arrived back home and resumed with the meal preparation. This time the other shoe had dropped, so to speak. The mood had saddened and we all were quiet. Eleven people were sharing this Thanksgiving meal. Gary's responsibility was to set the table. He was standing next to me counting out silverware. Suddenly he began to cry. I turned to him and asked what was wrong. It was such a silly question. He told me that an entire place setting was missing. The set contained settings for twelve people. Aaron would have had the twelfth person. He was missing and an entire set was missing. Gary believed that this was a sign from Aaron. I completely agreed. Aaron had a habit of bringing food into his room. He would carry a dish and silverware. Mysteriously, the silverware would never come back out of his room. It would disappear into the bowels of Aaron land. If Aaron could send a sign on Thanksgiving, a holiday completely about food, he would do something with the silverware. Gary looked at me and said, "You and your damn signs!" We were able to laugh. I was comforted.

We shared the meal with our loved ones. We ate, we cried, and we laughed. Time passed and we got through the day. In a life of surviving one day at a time, we managed to survive a difficult day.

Unbeknownst to us, a very special moment occurred that Thanksgiving Day. A very special person in my life experienced a spiritual moment that day. She was not able to share this with me until weeks later. However, I believe it needs to be told at this time. She was sitting at the end of the dinner table. All the guests were gathered around the table. At this time she was the only one facing in the direction of the living room window. Most of us were crying as we looked at a photo album. It was probably the saddest moment of that day. She looked up towards the window and saw someone standing in front of the window. There was a golden outline of a tall person. She was taken back by this image. It appeared to shimmer slightly and then moved toward Tilly, Aaron's beagle, who was sitting in a chair next to the window. It appeared that a person was moving toward Tilly and bending down to pet her. At that moment Tilly lifted her head and looked right into the direction of this form. The form faded, and the special person was so overcome with emotion that she had to leave the room. She believed that the form was Aaron. The form was the shape of a person and was tall. Looking back at that moment, I do remember her leaving the room for a while. She did not have the courage to describe what she saw. She thought she had lost her faculties for a moment. A couple of weeks after Thanksgiving, she managed to gather the strength to tell me her story. When she had described the event to me, I told her that she had described the image that Alyssa had captured on film. The more she recalled that day, the more she believed it was Aaron. We hugged and cried. The emotion is indescribable. This journey of seeking the proof of afterlife was rewarding me with the most incredible evidence.

There is more to this amazing story. About one year after this event, I arranged for a medium to come to my home. It was a group reading. At one point during the reading, the medium pointed to the living room window. He said, "He is pointing at the window to me. He is saying something about the window. He wants you to know that he was in the window."

Christmas

When I read these typed words, I am amazed all over again. Faith is the key factor. If I have faith, everything is all right with the world. If Aaron exists, everything is all right with the world. How can I ever doubt myself again? Every sign, every event deepens my faith and belief.

Christmas was in the air. Gary and I decorate the Friday after Thanksgiving and have done that every year since we said, "I do." There was no time to ponder Christmas. The morning after turkey day it was automatic to decorate the tree. We decided to continue with our traditions because of the girls. Normal routines can console the soul. We were going to keep to the Christmas traditions. Although the girls were our main concern, we still had another child to consider. It was important for us to also honor and recognize Aaron at this very special time of year. How could we keep with tradition and remember Aaron? We have always decorated the outside of the house with white lights. It was important for us to continue with the decorations, but my husband suggested that we put a small tree outside for Aaron. We came up with the idea to decorate the small tree with red lights. We could combine both the life before Aaron and the life after losing Aaron.

134

My brother-in-law made us a beautiful little wooden tree. We set the tree in the front yard next to the stairs. Gary strung red lights. That evening we lit the tree. We stood in the front yard gazing at the house and "Aaron's Tree." The house looked incredible. White lights sparkled. The red tree stood out like a beacon against the backdrop of white. A passerby would look at my house and see the little red tree. He might wonder why we chose to put a little red tree in the middle of all the white, but no explanation was needed. All who loved Aaron would know immediately that it was for my son. Gary and I were so proud. We kept to the Zabierek tradition and acknowledged Aaron.

Gary and I were returning home one night after Christmas shopping. We were discussing another challenge. Every year since Aaron's birth, I had sent Christmas cards with pictures of my children. One child was missing. What was I going to do this year? I was afraid that if I stopped sending the cards, it would be remembered that in the year that Aaron died, a classic Zabierek tradition also died. How could I send a picture of my beautiful girls and still honor Aaron? Suddenly an idea came to me. I could take a picture of the girls standing in front of the tree. It was a windy night with snowflakes swirling. This was a perfect backdrop for my picture. I would be able to show my family and friends a picture of my beautiful daughters and also acknowledge Aaron. I called the girls and asked them to be prepared to come outside to take a picture. When I arrived home, the girls were waiting for me. They both were dressed in blue jeans, a red sweatshirt and black gloves. I was so pleased and proud of them. I hadn't asked for the red sweatshirts. I placed them on either side of the tree. I snapped a few pictures before the cold and wind drove us inside. I hurried to my favorite Wal-Mart photo shop and developed the film. To my delight, the pictures were perfect. I chose a card and on the inside cover I secured the picture. I placed a caption under the tree that read "Aaron's Tree." The response I received from that card was incredibly positive. I was proud.

The Holiday

We proceeded with the shopping and all the preparations for the holiday. The actual purchasing of the gifts was very difficult for me. As I shopped, I would see a perfect gift for Aaron. It was automatic. I would pick it up, then realize that I could no longer buy gifts for him. The pain would spread throughout my body. It is not easy to turn around and continue on with the shopping. People are typically happy at that time of year. Who wants to see a crying woman in their midst? We shopped as little as we could.

Gary and I wanted to keep to the normal routine on Christmas. This included an open house on Christmas Eve and coffee in the morning with my parents and in-laws. We have done this since the kids were very small. It allowed the grandparents to see the gifts that Santa brought. We also wanted to change some of it, especially the parts that would show an obvious void. Of course, there would be an obvious void, but we anticipated some times to be harder than others. We decided to have the girls open their gifts on Christmas Eve. This would allow us time to attend mass on Christmas morning. Gary wanted to attend mass to pray for Aaron. Our plan was to go to church and proceed to the cemetery immediately after mass. We would light Aaron's candle. I liked this plan. It changed the routine slightly and added a distraction. The girls were not happy with this plan. Ironically they wanted to keep to the same routine. Gary and I decided to overrule them. It was hard to disappoint them, but we knew that the normal routine would be too difficult. If we attended mass, we would have to get ready earlier in the morning, thus we had a distraction. We chose this new plan.

The prelude to the main event was my family Christmas party. My family typically gathers the Saturday before Christmas to celebrate. I woke early on this day to prepare and received a surprise visit from my brother. He wanted to see us at the house before the family party. He knew the day was going to be difficult for us all and wanted to see us prior to the party. I love him for visiting us that day. He warmed my heart. I know the day was equally difficult for him. He and Aaron were very close. They were more like brothers than nephew and uncle. I realized that he also had suffered a tremendous loss when Aaron died. He lived alone and I believe this added to his pain. Aaron had spent a lot of time at his house, and he must have felt the emptiness just as we did. I was grateful that he recognized the fact that the day was going to be hard for us.

The day was very sad without Aaron. We cried at times but managed to survive the party without him. However, one moment does stand out in my mind. Alyssa wanted a picture of all the children. Nobody responded to her request and gathered the children. My sister stated that it would be too difficult for my mother to pose the kids without Aaron. I let the whole issue slide. Later that evening at home, Alyssa seemed sadder than she had been during the day. I asked her what was bothering her. Again, this was such a silly question. She was disappointed that we never gathered the kids and took a picture. I was sorry that I let her down. We talked about it. I began to feel bad that I did not honor her request. I realized that although the picture would have an empty seat, Alyssa needed the picture because it was the normal routine. She found comfort in the normal routines. I also realized that if we stopped taking pictures, the kids would not have any photos to look back on after Aaron died. They had a right to create memories. I did not want to eliminate this part of the holiday because Aaron was missing. I promised Alyssa that the next time we gathered as a family, I would take a picture of the kids. I also promised myself that I would not eliminate a tradition so that some day we would say to future generations, "We used to .... but when Aaron died we stopped." Memories are created for the living. Memories are a tool for healing. I also learned the importance of communicating and listening. We need to listen to each other's needs. If taking that picture helped heal Alyssa, then my pain was worth the price.

Countdown

Christmas was just days away. The countdown began. As each day passed, my nerves become more frazzled. I kept myself busy with the preparations. Cooking and cleaning were a great distraction. The anticipation is similar to a volcano about to erupt. You know that it is eventually going to erupt, but you do not know how large-scale the eruption will be. Since I am a "glass half empty" girl, I imagined the worst. This works in my favor on occasion. I have a very vivid imagination, and expecting the worst means that most likely the worst will not happen. When Christmas Eve arrived, I awoke with a sense of impending doom. It almost felt like the morning after Aaron died. The air was thick with sadness. I meandered through the morning with the usual preparations. The usual routine helped pass the time.

One Christmas tradition was especially important to Aaron. On Christmas Eve we break bread to honor the Polish heritage. My in-laws obtain the bread from a Polish church. Once all of our guests have arrived on Christmas Eve, we pass out a piece of bread to everyone. Each person takes a small piece of bread from someone else. Each person eats the piece taken, and Christmas greetings are exchanged. Aaron really enjoyed this tradition. How could we do this without him?

Gary came up with a solution. We could still break bread with Aaron! He suggested we go to the cemetery on Christmas Eve and break bread there with Aaron. Gary got one of the "Aaron's Tree" Christmas cards, a piece of bread and a ziplock bag. After the food preparations were complete and we were all ready for the guests to arrive, the four of us, along with my in-laws, went to the cemetery. Gary lit the candle. He gave each of us a piece of the bread. We broke pieces and exchanged greetings. We took the remaining piece of bread in our hands and wished Aaron a Merry Christmas as we placed our piece of bread in the card. Gary sealed the card inside the plastic bag. He placed the bag on Aaron's grave. I stood and looked at my family. Tears streamed down our faces. It was a bittersweet moment. The sadness overwhelmed me, but I believed that Aaron was smiling down on us. He would be happy that we intended to continue with the breaking of the bread and had found a way to include him in his favorite Polish tradition on Christmas Eve.

We returned home to wait for the guests. It was a somber mood. I must have repaired my eye make up ten times. Because I refused to be seen without wearing my eye make-up, I spent all my time in the bathroom. It probably would have been easier to skip the make-up, but, alas, I am too vain. Aaron was probably laughing at me every time I repaired it. He was a no-nonsense guy and would have voted for the natural look. I can smile about it now.

Just before the guests arrived, the telephone rang. My girlfriend was on the line. A snowstorm was expected Christmas Day. Her family lived on the Cape and was supposed to travel to her house and share dinner on Christmas Day. They had just called her and cancelled the trip. They were afraid to drive up north in the bad weather. She had already prepared most of the food and had enough to feed an army. She invited us to dinner. Gary and I discussed it and decided to accept her invitation. Because we shared Christmas dinner with my in-laws and Gary's aunt, they would join us as well. The weather couldn't stop us because we only lived across town. Gary and I thought about it. This was another change in the routine. By going to my girlfriend's house we would be doing something completely different. There would not be an empty seat at my house. Did Aaron arrange the storm and set the stage for this welcome change? Once again my extraordinary son was hard at work.

**Christmas Eve and Christmas Day**

The guests began to arrive. As people came in, I could see the sympathy in their eyes. This will forever bother me, but I am glad that everyone could come to my home. The hustle and bustle of evening distracted us all. We enjoyed the meal and the company. Everyone was talking about the impending storm. It was a relief to focus on the snow. The evening passed quickly. "Get through it," was the new motto of the Zabierek household.

When the last of the guests had departed, the four of us gathered to open the gifts. It was strange to be opening the gifts on this evening. Usually Alyssa would rush to bed so that the morning would arrive quicker. She would ask my brother and his wife to tuck her in just before they left. She would tell them about her wish list. The child in her would radiate through the house, as the sun brightens the day. I missed her excitement and joy. We sat near the tree. It was very quiet. Part of me wanted to run out the front door. This was going to be extremely difficult. Aaron was gone. His spot was empty. Nothing would ever change that. Even though it was not Christmas morning, the pain was not lessened. I had fooled myself into believing that if we did the gift exchange completely differently, it would lessen the pain. I was wrong.

Gary selected a gift for each of them. The opening began. I looked at my daughters with incredible love. I wanted to hold them and never let go. I could not protect them from the pain. That was harder to deal with than my own pain. I was frozen in my chair and watched my daughters. As they opened more gifts, a trickle of joy seeped in. I could see some happiness. I realized that this is what it was all about. They are alive and here with me. I had to set aside the pain and let them be children. I wanted their memories to be happy. The last thing Gary and I wanted for our children was the elimination of Christmas. They needed to continue with the happy times. Life was so sad for us we needed joy in our hearts again. I try to imagine Aaron hovering over the girls. He had to be here with us, I thought to myself. I wanted my family complete and this was the only way to have what I wanted.

When the girls had finished opening their gifts, they were completely exhausted. They went to bed. As they said goodnight to us, I hoped the sleep would calm them and take away some of the sadness. Gary and I straightened the house. Just before going to bed we filled the stockings. The girls wanted to save those for Christmas morning. It was something to look forward to. We hung them by the fire. Aaron's was missing. A tear rolled down my cheek. Gary and I hugged. As parents, we had never imagined we would lose our firstborn child. As I crawled into bed, the tears streamed down my face. I begged for sleep to take over. I prayed for God to give me the strength I needed to survive Christmas Day.

Christmas Morning

The morning arrived fast. I awoke tired to the bone, but at least my eyes were dry. I thanked the Lord. I left my family sleeping and took my shower. Once Gary and I had finished getting ready, we woke up the girls. Ashley and Alyssa wanted to open their stockings. There was a little bit of joy on this day. I am glad we saved the stockings for the morning. Everybody seemed to be doing all right. We left for church. The day did not feel very much like Christmas to me. It was very different from what I had been accustomed to. Changing the routine helped, but it was a very difficult day. The special days seem to bring the anger to the surface as well as the sadness. The fact that Aaron is missing is unjust to me. I have been robbed. What did I do in my past to be punished in this way? When I have those thought, I force myself to think of something else. I was not being punished; Aaron's death was an accident.

As I sat in church, these angry feelings began to surface again. I looked at my surroundings and realized where I was. I started to feel ashamed. I was in God's home. It was a place of beauty and love. I thought of a mother at one of my support groups. She believed that her son was in a beautiful, loving place. She wouldn't change places with her son because he was in a better place. As I thought of this mother, I looked at the beauty around me, the stained glass windows, the statues, and the people. So many were gathered before God. I thought of God. I have been taught that God equally loves everybody. I have been told to live my life with the expectation of joining him when I die. How could I be angry? My faith has taught me that life continues after this world. The people around me were proof of that. Every sign from Aaron came flooding into my memories. I thought of the dragonflies, dreams, soccer balls, the angel in the clouds, the pictures at the scene of the accident, Wal-Mart and my aunt's vision. I had proof in my own back yard! I thought of my extraordinary son. This was a turning point for me. At that moment, on Christmas Day, I remembered my faith and believed.

Connecting with Mom

The Christmas present that Gary and I gave my parents and my in-laws were tickets to see a concert performed by the Boston Pops Orchestra. A week after Christmas we took the four of them to the concert. My dad arranged for a limousine ride. It began as a wonderful evening. The air was crisp. We drove into the big city in luxury. The radio was on in the limousine. As I sat with my family, trumpet sounds flowed from the radio. This was music to my ears. Aaron was with us. I was happy.

We arrived at Symphony Hall. It was a treat to step out of that limousine! We found our seats and waited excitedly for the show to begin. I sat next to my mother. We started talking about Aaron and the meaning of the afterlife. It seemed natural to talk about Aaron at a band concert. We had spent so many nights and weekends following the Methuen High Band. I talked about the books that I was reading. As I told them about some of the things that I had read about the afterlife, I started to see a gleam in their eyes. I was seeing hope in their eyes. As they listened to me talk, they were beginning to feel hopeful that Aaron lived on. Wasn't this what it was all about? Hope to be reunited with their grandson. Hope that Aaron lived on.

During a pause in the conversation, my mother quietly spoke to me. She thought she had experienced a sign. She wanted to tell me her story. I was an eager listener. She began her story. She had been sitting in the living room with my father. My brother had left the house an hour earlier. The weather was bad, and she was worried about his drive home. Wanting him to arrive home safely, she prayed to Aaron. She asked Aaron to guide him home. As she sat there feeling very anxious, the telephone rang. My brother called to say that he had made it safely home. She breathed a sigh of relief and thanked Aaron. As she was thanking Aaron, she turned to the Christmas tree. An ornament caught her eye. This ornament seemed to stand out. As she looked at the ornament, it appeared brighter than the other ornaments on the tree. It seemed to glow. The ornament began to radiate a bright blue aura! The color was brighter than any she'd ever seen. She was utterly taken back by what she saw. She was immediately filled with peace and joy. As she told me this story, I experienced a tingling feeling. I had goose bumps all over my body. She had asked my father if he saw this sign and he did not. She thought because she saw it alone that it might not have existed. I was overjoyed. My mom hadn't read the books I had. She couldn't have known that she had witnessed a sign from a spirit. All the books I have read describe a radiating light, with colors brighter than any color seen on earth, being sent by spirits. My Mom had never heard about that. She was touched deeply. My father was also amazed. At that moment the concert began. Trumpets echoed throughout the magnificent hall, and I knew that I had an extraordinary son.

What's Next?

Could it really be over? Did we survive the holidays? I asked myself these questions every day. It appeared to be true. The aroma of cinnamon and evergreen no longer permeated the house. The tree was gone. The trimmings were taken down. The glitter and sparkle were replaced with a vast, flat, empty room. I missed the festive atmosphere. Although we should have been proud to survive Christmas, the emptiness reminded me that Aaron was gone. The hustle and bustle of the holidays had been a distraction. What is next?

I did have an event that should have distracted me. Ashley's birthday was a few weeks away. This was a happy time for her. She was turning eighteen years old. It was a milestone for her. For me it was a reminder that Aaron would no longer have birthdays to celebrate. The day would come, but he would be missing. Could I wipe October 21st from the calendar for the rest of my days on earth? Why couldn't we go from October 20th to October 22nd? Unfortunately I was not Harry Potter. Therefore, I did not have a magic wand to wave around and erase a painful day for me. I also could not overshadow Ashley's day by mourning Aaron. She deserved a birthday. Children, especially mine, love their birthdays. We have always made each birthday special.

I remembered Aaron's words from the first medium visit, "We are still role models to these children. Even though we might be guiding them through life we have to demonstrate to them that we still have the ability to celebrate life." I was determined to celebrate Ashley's birthday.

Gary has always been a generous husband and father. However, since Aaron's death he has become more generous with the girls. We celebrated Ashley's birthday with great success for her. Because we had changed the tradition, Alyssa joined us for dinner. Alyssa was glad of the change. Ashley was too, although I know deep down inside she really wanted her parents alone. Gary and I are insistent to avoid anything that will sadden our children. We did make a commitment with each other to guarantee quality time with both of our daughters. We refuse to create times that will eventually cause regret with our daughters.

Finding a Focus

As long as I had an event to focus on, the days passed without incident. I needed to keep busy. I have always been one to fill every minute of the day. I plan to the extreme. I drive my family crazy. Aaron was the opposite of me. He never planned. He was very laid back and casual. His motto was that if you could put it off until tomorrow you could really put if off for two days. He would laugh at me when I made my lists. He thought I should keep the list in my mind. That was easy for him to say. He had a photographic memory! He thought it was a waste of time to write it down and follow the list. He surprised me one day. I thought I had him figured out until he actually imitated me. His girlfriend wanted to have a party. He talked about the party for a couple of days. One night he was on the phone with her and was very agitated. The party was a few days away, and she had not planned anything yet. I could hear him tell her to make a list of people she expected to come. He also told her to think of the food and drink that she would like to serve. He sounded like me. I smiled. Years of watching me plan had taught him well. He would never admit it, but he did not think it was frivolous to plan after all. This memory makes me smile.

Ashley was a focus in other ways. She was preparing to graduate from high school. This was a major event in her life. Ironically, the month that she would be graduating was the same month as the anniversary of Aaron's death. A celebration and a solemn event would occur in the same month. One could be a distraction, yet the other would certainly overshadow everything. The infamous dark cloud was just beginning to float in the direction of my house. I forced myself to concentrate on Ashley. If I made her a priority, I could keep the dark cloud at bay.

Trudging Along

As the time passed, I focused on the events that lay ahead. When I had bad days, I would make myself focus on the future. I busied myself with lists. I was giving my son a reason to smile at me. My birthday came and went. Don't get me wrong, Gary and the girls made my day very special. As I stated earlier, my husband is very generous. However, this was the first birthday that I did not want to celebrate. I think I felt guilty. Aaron could no longer have birthdays so I should not. I also thought of the day Aaron died. He died the day before Gary's birthday. On my birthday I thought of my husband. How could he ever celebrate his birthday again? I wanted the day to pass quickly so that I could continue to plan.

Shortly after my birthday, Easter was upon us. It was another holiday to worry about. My family was coming to my house for dinner. Gary and I wanted to be the hosts. Once again, if we were cooking and cleaning, we would not think of Aaron. The holiday was easier for me than my husband. He had a difficult day. I remember seeing him break down as he carved the ham. My sister followed him and spent some time with him. The remaining guests had no idea of the drama unfolding. I did not want to bring everybody down. I feel bad about that now. I should have followed my husband. I know now that I did not follow him because I wanted the day to be happy. If I had gone to him, I would have cried with him. I cannot be strong when one of my own is suffering. My sister did a great job of comforting Gary. I finished with the ham, and dinner commenced. Gary was fine the rest of the day. He was as fine as one can be after losing a child. Another day crossed off the calendar and back to my planning.

The Oasis

A parched traveler lost in the desert with no hope sees a water fountain on the horizon. The fountain could be real or imaginary, but it gives the lonely traveler hope and renewed strength. Gary and I were travelers lost in the desert. One day on our long journey, each of us saw an oasis on the horizon.

It was a weekday early in the morning. I climbed into my car and headed out for a day at the office. I stopped my car at the end of the driveway and looked for approaching traffic. Something caught my eye on the driver's side of the car. On the side of the road just to the left of my driveway sat a soccer ball! It was a very worn soccer ball. I smiled and thought of Aaron. I began my Angel day. As I drove to work, I thought of the soccer ball. How did it get there? Where did it come from? There were no children on my street in the vicinity of where the ball was. I live on a tree-lined country road. I can not imagine how this ball ended up in my driveway. As I continued with my day, I thought of that ball and Aaron every minute. What started out as another begrudging day at the office turned into a day of hope. When my work day finished, I began to look forward to seeing the soccer ball again. As I drove home, the anticipation started to build. I looked forward to seeing that wonderful worn ball. I turned onto my street and headed to my house. As I made the approach to my driveway, I looked for the ball. It was gone! My heart sank. At that moment all the joy and happiness I had felt that day slipped away. I parked the car, gathered my things and walked to the front door. I stepped on the walkway and stopped in my tracks. Sitting by my front door was the soccer ball! A wave of joy and hope seeped throughout my body. I stood there looking at this soccer ball and asked the same questions I had asked earlier. How did it get here? My driveway is a slight incline. Halfway down the driveway a second circular drive veers off the main driveway. This ball had not only rolled down the drive but also turned onto the second drive. I looked at the ball, and the following words rang in my head and my heart, "Hi Mum."

Gary's Angel day was much more amazing than mine. I will never forget the day when my husband called me at work with an incredible story. Ironically, his day had started out just the same as mine. He was on his way to work. He drives a half-hour north to his office. This particular day he was thinking of Aaron. He was on the highway looking ahead with thoughts of Aaron on his mind. As he gazed out of the windshield, something caught his eye straight ahead. A dragonfly was flying just ahead of his car! The car was traveling at sixty-five miles an hour. The dragonfly was a beacon leading the way. He followed that dragonfly for five minutes! The hope and joy in my husband's voice as he recited his story was amazing. Both of these events had a profound effect on the two of us. To this day that soccer ball is sitting in my yard. I did question every family member to ask if they had moved the ball. All replied, "No." Some days the soccer ball appears in a different spot. It could be the wind, but I believe Aaron and the spirits are playing soccer. Gary and I do have an extraordinary son.

Ashley's Big Day

Time continued to pass. Surviving each day was an accomplishment. The sun rose and set as the days passed. There were cloudy days and sunny days. There were more cloudy days than sunny days but we managed to get through it. Everything I read states the first year is the hardest. Each time an event passed, I felt like a child completing a semester of school. The passing of each semester brings a child closer to the summer. I was that child looking forward to summer.

The end of the first year, however, meant that we had to face the anniversary of Aaron's death. There were two major events approaching. Ashley was graduating from high school, and Aaron's anniversary was close behind. My goal was to keep the events separate and focus on Ashley's graduation. I did not want her day to be overshadowed by Aaron's day. However, try as I might, both events had something in common. During Ashley's graduation, the first scholarship for Aaron would be handed out. It had never occurred to me that Aaron would end up being the focus on Ashley's graduation day. It is a key lesson that I have learned. I can't hide from my grief and I can't separate the grief. Aaron was a part of our lives and will be a part of us forever.

Aaron's Scholarship

Aaron's scholarship was growing by leaps and bounds. Because this would be the first year it would be awarded and Ashley was graduating, she asked to present Aaron's scholarship. Gary and I agreed with her. It was ironic that we would honor Aaron while celebrating Ashley. It is strange how things work out. Maybe they really are planned that way? On our behalf the Band Director investigated the possibility of Ashley presenting the scholarship. It never occurred to us that our request would be declined. However, it was indeed declined. With the large number of scholarships, it was decided that by allowing Ashley to present, a precedent would be set and all future requests would have to be honored. Gary and I discussed this at length. Surely by allowing Ashley to present Aaron's scholarship a precedent would not be established. How many students would lose a sibling the same year that they graduated? I was very upset by the decision. I decided to write a letter to the superintendent of the school department.

My letter caused much discussion and a change in plans, to our delight. The officials involved agreed with us and wanted to find a way to honor our request. An award ceremony was scheduled prior to graduation. The purpose of the ceremony was to highlight specific scholarships and present academic awards. Aaron's scholarship would be presented at this ceremony. The Band Director would give a speech about the scholarship, and Ashley would actually present the scholarship to the recipient. This was the perfect solution. Ashley was already invited to the ceremony. She was to be honored for her own academic achievements. The evening would be bittersweet. As Ashley was honored, Aaron would also be honored.

When the evening arrived, we invited the immediate family to attend. As we sat in that auditorium, I remembered all the times we had sat there for Aaron. Memories came flooding back to me. I struggled to hold the tears at bay. The program began. Aaron's scholarship was presented toward the middle of the evening. The Band Director gave his tribute to Aaron. He spoke eloquently, proudly, and emotionally. Ashley had told me that she was not nervous. I was nervous for her. I watched her closely. The courage it must have taken for her to stand beside the director as he spoke about her brother. She was in control initially. As he continued to talk, her reserve broke down. Her eyes seemed to glisten, and I realized that she was beginning to cry. The tears simmering inside of me reached a boiling point and spilled over. I watched my daughter's tears also begin to stream down her face. I had to restrain myself from running to the stage and gathering her into my arms. I wanted to stop her pain. An unknown force must have kept me in my chair. My heart was broken again. I sat in agony until the speech was finished. Between Ashley's suffering and the grown man's emotional voice, there was not a dry eye in the room. As Ashley was experiencing the same raw pain that we experienced the night that Aaron died, the audience was witnessing her pain. It had to be difficult to stand on that stage. I am sure she wanted to run off the stage. The same force that held me in my chair was holding her on the stage. Finally the recipient was called to the stage. Ashley gathered what strength was left inside and handed the award to Aaron's fellow band member. He gathered her in a very tender hug. At that moment I was overwhelmed with pride for my daughter. I had a revelation. She and her sister were the reason that Gary and I got out of bed every morning. This was our reward. An amazing young woman was standing on stage before us, and we had another amazing young woman in the wings. This is parenting at its best. Every time Gary and I forced ourselves to trudge along was because of the girls. It paid off. Our extraordinary son was evolving to our extraordinary children.

When the ceremony was completely over, the principal sought us out. She gave us her sympathy and apologized for denying our initial request to have Ashley hand out the scholarship. She was very kind and compassionate. The recipient also came over to us. His words still ring clear in my head. He said, "Thank you for the scholarship. I promise to make the big guy proud."

Alyssa

Alyssa was graduating from the eighth grade. As part of the celebration of completing grammar school, the class was partaking in a trip to New York. Aaron and Ashley had both taken a similar type of class trip. Unfortunately the trip was the week prior to Ashley's graduation. Alyssa's class would return home the day of the graduation. Alyssa was very upset by this. She was afraid that she would miss Ashley's graduation, and she refused to miss the graduation. She wanted to support her sister and also witness the first presentation of Aaron's scholarship. She had to miss the award ceremony and shed many tears over it. She would not miss this special day. Gary decided that he would drive to New York the second-to-last day of the trip. He would stay in the same hotel as Alyssa, and this would enable him to take her home first thing in the morning. The car would take less time to drive home than the bus would. He is a dedicated parent and will stop at nothing for his children. I still think of him driving alone for eight hours, followed by another eight hours in the car with four teenage girls! When other parents heard about Gary's trip, parents with a child graduating and a younger one on the trip asked Gary if he would consider an additional passenger. He agreed to three such passengers.

His dedication as a parent was always a quality to be admired. His commitment to continue to be a parent in the absence of his eldest son drove him with a purpose possessed by few.

Ashley prepared for one of the most important days of her life. She was beautiful and I sensed a strength that few her age possess. Often times when a tragedy occurs, one is asked to look for the good in the situation. I would ask myself how any good could possibly come out of my son's death? I guess now I perceive Ashley's strength and Alyssa's dedication to her sister as the good in my personal tragedy. Love seeped into my bones as I watched my daughter while I waited for my youngest child and my husband.

They arrived in the nick of time. Alyssa raced to change and we were off to the ceremony. It was a proud moment for Gary and me. The night was bittersweet once again. Not so long ago we had sat in the same bleachers for our first-born. Now our second child was achieving the same goal of completing high school. The journey of life is similar to a highway with many off ramps. As a parent, one dreams of her children progressing on this highway. A child may select an off ramp, but he or she will eventually get back on. It is never imagined that a child stops the journey halfway through. I also imagine that siblings have the same expectations. Not only were we given a tough road, but Ashley was also given a tough road. We were strong for her. She did us proud. Ashley received six scholarships, to our delight. A grand event, with a Hawaiian theme, was planned for Ashley. We also had decided to take her out to dinner at a lovely restaurant to celebrate the evening of graduation. We had double the reason to celebrate. We complied with Aaron's wishes, spoken that day through the medium. We gave Ashley a special night to remember, just as we had given one to Aaron.

Alyssa's Big Day

"Stop the roller coaster; I want to get off," I said in my mind daily. Much to my dismay, the roller coaster did not have a stop button. As Aaron's anniversary approached, I did not want to think about it or anything else for that matter. I wanted to stop the roller coaster. I have said over and over again that my children are a blessing. In this case it is absolutely true. There was a bonus here as well. The girls were a blessing and a distraction. The girls were proof that the roller coaster had to continue and would never stop. Ashley's graduation demonstrated that life would still move down that highway, yet it provided a distraction for us. We focused on Ashley and the graduation so much that it kept that black hole from being the center of our lives. Alyssa's eighth grade graduation would be another welcome distraction.

It was a simple ceremony. One we had done twice before. Our last child was following the path of her elder siblings. It was a joyous occasion, though slightly overshadowed. Aaron had not attended the same grammar school. This fact made it easier for us. I brought my video camera. As the children processed into the hall, I could see the joy and excitement in Alyssa's eyes. She was happy. Her young years allowed her to bury the pain more easily than her parents could. I was grateful for that. I filmed her and we all clapped for Alyssa. We managed to appear as all the parents in that auditorium, proud and happy. Alyssa would not look back on that day and remember any shadows. We were creating memories important to her success.

As the ceremony came to a close, two special awards were to be given. The awards were called "Team Teacher Award." The teachers chose a boy and girl that would receive this award. The recipient would be presented with a very distinguished honor. The teachers had selected a boy and girl student with many qualities, including leadership, excellent academic skills, teamwork, and, above all, role model to all students. The girl's award was presented first. I turned my camera on and focused on the teacher. I thought that it could be one of Alyssa's friends, and I wanted to capture the moment for her. I turned to the teacher and listened as she said, "And this year's girl Team Teacher Award goes to Alyssa Zabierek." Tears welled inside my eyes, spilling over. I reached for Gary's hand while I cried. My heart filled with love. Alyssa and Ashley were succeeding. We were still the parents we were prior to Aaron's death. We had raised an extraordinary son and were continuing to raise remarkable daughters. All the times that we buried our pain for the sake of the girls were paying off. This moment combined with Ashley's success gave us the conviction that we needed to continue down that highway of life.

Let The Preparations Begin

The year was coming to a close. I would have never imagined that I could survive this past year. The days of wanting my own life to end have passed slowly, yet the year is almost over. I remember the emotions and pain on the day that I lost my son. The morning after, I gazed at my reflection in the mirror. I wanted to pick up a lipstick and write on that mirror, thirty-eight years left to go until I meet Aaron again. In the blink of an eye, I transformed from a woman who was afraid to die and wanted to live forever, to a woman who thought of living as a chore and death as a welcome invitation. I vowed to count down my days left on earth.

I look in that mirror today and I see that number changing to thirty-seven. I see a different woman. I can't say that I have completely given up the idea of wishing my life away. As that number appears before my eyes, the faces of my children also appear. I think of Aaron's words to be the same mother for my girls as I was to him. I think of my daughters and their struggles. I am a Mom. This is the first line in my character description. A mother takes care of her children. I take care of Aaron by praying the rosary, lighting his candle, and tending to his grave. I take care of my daughters by giving them love and support. I also physically care for my daughters as well as provide a home for them. If I leave earth early, although I would be with Aaron, I would not be able to do more for him. He is with the heavenly Father. However, if I leave early, my girls would be without a mother. I would fail as a Mom. Life was a scale for me, balancing precariously between living and leaving. Aaron's choice and my choice were tipping that scale to the living. I let the number fade from the mirror.

Unfortunately with the anniversary of Aaron's death just weeks away, that scale was teetering. The living side of the scale held the accomplishment of surviving the past eleven months and the faces of my daughters and husband. The living side also held the task of repeating the day I had lost my first-born son. This one fact was causing the scale to tip in the direction of leaving. How could I relive that fateful day? Would the pain be as intense as it was? The scale tipped precariously. The faces of Alyssa, Ashley, and Gary began to shine through. I could help them more that I could help Aaron. I imagined their pain if I left, and suddenly there was no choice for me. I belonged with the living. There would be decades of June thirtieths. This one would be that hardest. Without a magic wand I would have to live through this day and maintain the balance on the scale. I prayed to Aaron for strength.

The Anniversary

Gary and I discussed the anniversary. We came to the decision that we had two choices to handle the day. The first choice was to let the day come and go, hoping for it to pass quickly. The second choice was to hold a memorial mass and pray for Aaron with family and friends. As we discussed the choices, we both realized that there was only one decision to be made. We chose to honor Aaron and arrange for a memorial mass. We both have deepened our faith in God and the church. The old adage states that prayer is powerful. We needed to pray for our son. We wanted to publicly state this to Aaron. We also wanted to give our family and friends the opportunity to see us again. We needed to thank everyone for their love and support. This mass would allow us the opportunity to accomplish our goals.

Let the Planning Begin

Planning is what my husband and I do best. Remember those lists I mentioned earlier? I furiously made lists. The church and priest were the easy part. Of course, it would be St. Monica's with Father David serving the mass. We contacted Father David and his response was filled with joy and honor. He wanted to be the one to celebrate and honor Aaron's life in the house of God. We chose to have a private mass for family and friends, and Father David agreed. We selected the day prior to the anniversary because most people would be available, as it was a Sunday. He called the church on our behalf. The church was available and the first step was taken.

We immediately began to talk about the invitation list, music, food, readings, etc. There appeared to be lots to decide and do. This was turning out to be the best distraction. With all of the planning to do, there was little time to think. Gary and I pulled out the guest book from Aaron's wake. This is where we gathered the invitation list. We included everyone who had an impact on our lives and Aaron's life. Surprisingly, the list grew to be two hundred and fifty long. Where would we put all of these people if we were to feed them, and how in the world would we feed them all? Our parents were involved in the planning, and it was suggested that we use the same hall that the mercy meal had been held in. After contacting my uncle, we booked the hall and were on our way.

In a flurry of activity, I designed the invitations on my computer at home, addressed them, and off they went to the post office. As I dropped them into the box, a little bit of pride seeped into my weary bones. I wanted the world to know that my family survived. I was proud that my husband and I had committed to this mass. Aaron would be proud of us too. I thought of it as giving him a chance to visit with everyone who impacted his life, at the same time. A little bit of me was angry that it wasn't a college graduation or a wedding. However, this was the hand we were dealt and it was our duty to plan, celebrate, and honor him just as if we were planning that graduation or wedding.

The girls also rose to the occasion. Both of them decided to do a reading. Gary and I were overwhelmed with pride. We have strong, amazing young women. They also surprised us a second time. They heard me talking about handing out a token of remembrance at the mass. I wanted to give everyone a little something to remember Aaron. I thought of the spiritual cards that were handed out at the wake, and I wanted something similar for this occasion. Together they wrote a poem honoring their brother.

His smile shone bright,
His size was quite a sight.
We loved the way he
Laughed loudly,
He cared and loved
Everyone fondly.
He was smart and funny
To the end.
Dragonflies from heaven
Is what he sends.

> ***We know he's always***
> ***Around***
> ***Everywhere just waiting***
> ***To be found.***
> ***We continue each day***
> ***Knowing he's there.***
> ***Aaron we can feel you***
> ***Blowing through our hair.***
>
> ***Written with love from***
> ***Ashley & Alyssa***

I decided to make a bookmark with the poem. I wanted to place the black and white picture of Aaron at the top and surround the poem with dotted lines leading to a dragonfly on the bottom. This picture would represent the happy side of Aaron, and I know that is how he would want people to remember him. By adding the dragonfly, this symbol would be known to all. I was fortunate to have a cousin who worked in graphic design. He materialized my vision. I don't think he realizes how much he helped me by creating this bookmark, that he called an easy job. I will forever thank him when I look at the bookmark.

Music was a large part of Aaron's life, especially the times he played the trumpet in the church. Gary and I both agreed that the trumpet players from the funeral mass had to return and play for Aaron again. Luckily, they were available and quickly agreed to play for Aaron a second time. We also hired the Music Director at the church. She also was honored. Aaron had played with her many times in the church. Gary selected special songs for his son. It was all coming together. Every time we crossed an item off the list, we were closer to our goal of hosting a special memorial to our son.

The last item on my list was food. What were we going to feed these people? I pictured myself making five hundred meatballs and sighed heavily. Actually I probably screamed out loud! My husband's job allowed him access to food vendors and an opportunity to purchase food in bulk and at a low cost. He approached his Food Service Director and asked her for some meal suggestions. She turned out to be an angel. Not only did she have fabulous ideas, but she offered to make and serve the meal herself. She was willing to give her time and several of her staff jumped at the opportunity to assist her. Gary was overwhelmed. I was not surprised. Every time I attended one of his work functions, staff approached me and sang his praises. I have heard over and over again that he is the best boss around. It was at this point that my parents offered to pay for the meal. We were doubly blessed.

The event was planned and with special attention to detail. Gary and I were happy. This mass was giving us an opportunity to unite and fulfill our parenting roles. This ominous day was approaching fast, yet we have something very positive to look forward to.

Public Remembrance

We chose to put a first-year anniversary notice in the local newspaper. I was having difficulty selecting a message. Nothing seemed appropriate. I was in my house and I was wandering through each room looking at all of the pictures of Aaron. I often look at each picture, touch them and kiss them. The pictures placed around the house are easy to look at. I still have difficulty looking at pictures that I haven't seen for a while. Whenever I see a picture of Aaron that I haven't seen recently, sadness floods in and takes my breath away. Familiar faces soothe, new faces hurt. As I looked at the happy photo of Aaron, a plaque caught my eye. My mother-in-law had given me a framed poem recently. The poem was spoken by an individual who had passed away. She was touched by the poem and it reminded her of Aaron. The poem was from an individual asking his loved ones not to mourn. Aaron would have no patience for people who spent time mourning. He would speak the same words to us.

As I read the poem, I immediately knew that this must be the message I put in the newspaper. At the medium session, Aaron told us that he does not go to the grave. The medium stated, "He goes with you when you go there. Otherwise, he does not spend any time there." This poem captured Aaron's message.

We're Ready

With the planning complete, we had nothing to do but wait. The week prior to the anniversary was similar to the week prior to Aaron's wake. I asked myself some of the same questions. Would the girls be all right? How would I react to people? How would we survive the day? I stopped myself. Maybe Aaron stopped me, but I started to realize that this waiting period was entirely different. For starters, none of us were taking medication. We all were sleeping at night. We all looked healthier than that week prior to the wake. Most importantly, the four of us were still together as a family. I thought of that second day when I remembered the Life Time movies, where families would disintegrate after a tragedy. We were strong. I had kept my promise and held my family together as least for this first year. My daughters were healthy and amazing. My husband and I were still married and stronger than ever before. I was proud. As difficult as this past year had been, we had survived. If we could survive this past year, we could survive the Mass and the anniversary.

The Mass

I awoke just as I did for all of the "firsts" this past year. I lay in bed and hesitated to move. The quiet of morning is always so peaceful. I wanted to lie there forever. Unfortunately, I could not. Many people were waking that day with the anticipation of seeing my family and honoring Aaron. I had no choice. One step at a time, I thought to myself. I proceeded to make myself beautiful, if that is possible! I woke Gary and my girls. The mood was somber as we all prepared. There were no tears, just quiet. I think we all were waiting for the other shoe to drop. It did not. The time arrived to leave for the church. I watched Gary lock the front door. He was a strong loving man. I was blessed to have him in my life. I would not have survived this loss without him by my side. I thanked God. I looked at my beautiful girls. They were also strong and loving. Their success this past year was my strength. They gave me the desire and means to survive. I thanked God again.

We were the first to arrive in the church parking lot. The day was beautiful, just like the day that Aaron left us. We were too anxious to sit in the car so we all got out. I noticed cars parked right in front of the church entrance and realized that there was a funeral still in process. I thought this was so ironic. Suddenly one of the cars caught my attention. It was a police car. The fact that it was a police car was not what caught my eye, but the town painted on the side of the car is what caught my attention. Not only was a funeral held the same day as Aaron's memorial, but the police car was from Pelham, NH. Was this some kind of sign? People may think of me as morbid, but I do believe that this was a sign. Aaron died in Pelham, NH. He had a police escort at his funeral. It was more than a coincidence.

The funeral ended and we entered the church. Gary had ordered a basket of red roses to place at the altar. Red roses now represent Aaron. We also brought Aaron's high school graduation picture to place next to the roses at the altar. As I said, every detail was taken care of by my husband. The girls, Gary, and I sat in the same pew that we had sat in for the funeral. I was in disbelief that one year had passed since I had sat in that pew on the day I had buried my son. I can remember shutting my eyes, hoping to wake up from a horrific dream. I opened my eyes. It was not a dream. I looked around at the people entering the church. There were so many friendly and caring faces. The pity was gone from their eyes. It was replaced with love. I could see this clearly. Warmth seeped into my bones. We were doing the right thing. I felt good about this mass.

Father David entered the church and the mass began. We listened to his prayers as we held hands. It was a struggle to stay composed for all of us. Heaviness settled on our shoulders. Then the tears began. This time around, they seemed to stream more quietly and slowly. The raw pain, that had been held at bay for so long, surfaced.

It was time for my girls to stand and read their respective selections. I held my breath. I would not have had the strength to perform this task. I know my girls agreed to do it out of loyalty for their brother. Needless to say, there was not a dry eye in the church. Although the tears flowed, pride overwhelmed me. Ashley and Alyssa were honoring their brother in the most amazing fashion. The courage they possessed lifted my spirit. I imagined the day that I would tell this story to my future grandchildren. They planted the seed of hope.

It was now time for Father David to give his sermon. I held my girls tightly and focused on Father David. His love for Aaron was evident at he spoke so eloquently about my son. He told many stories and gave us a laugh or two. This time I could hear everything he was saying, unlike at the funeral mass. I absorbed every word, and then he told a story that caused me to sit up straight in the pew as my grandmother had taught me. He began to talk about signs from Heaven. He spoke the most beautiful words to a very attentive audience. He told my dragonfly story! This Catholic priest was describing our dragonfly encounters to everyone. I knew Father David listened to my stories, but I was unsure if he believed them. This was a testimony for me that he did believe. This captive audience was intently listening as he described our sign. There were over two hundred people in that church. Every time they encountered a dragonfly, they would think of Aaron. What more could a mother ask for? Aaron's memory would be perpetuated by so many.

When the mass concluded, Gary insisted on holding a receiving line for the four of us. He wanted to stand at the back of the church so that he could personally thank everyone. I was unsure about this idea, but I am glad that he insisted. Every person in that church stopped to see each one of us. As the people hugged me, I was again uplifted. Each hug strengthened me. Through the many arms around me, love penetrated to my soul. This was the medicine that I needed. Through hugs, tears, words of comfort and love, we thanked every single person in the church.

When the last hug was given, we proceeded to the hall to join our guests for the meal. As I walked through the door, I could not believe my eyes. The hall was filled with people, so that there was standing room only. We were all amazed! The air was almost visible as the love and support permeated. That very moment was more healing than any drug we could have been given. I scanned the room. Every table was adorned with a fresh red flower. As I looked closely, the flower held a tiny, wire dragonfly. The buffet table was just as amazing. China dishes lined the table. Each was filled with aromatic, delicious food. Gary's Food Service Director had surpassed my expectations. I closed my eyes, took a deep breath, and believed that I could survive.

The afternoon proved to be a strength-building session for all four of us. We dined and visited with all of our closest family members and friends. People, we did not expect to attend, attended the meal. Conversations were meaningful, silly, and absolutely enjoyable. For the first time in the past year, we all were close to being happy. So many "Aaron" stories were told to us and by us. Every person in the room was touched by the dragonfly stories and especially the girls' memento. Aaron would be proud of this day. I believe that our intention of showing our son, family, and friends that we were survivors was demonstrated greatly.

Regretfully, the day came to a close and it was time to leave. We visited the cemetery before going home. This saddened the mood a little. We wanted to leave the basket of red roses at his grave. Tears always flowed freely when we were all together at the grave. I believed those tears were less sad than the ocean of tears that fell before this day. We said our goodbyes as each one of us kissed the stone. I thanked my son and asked him to send me strength so that I could survive the next day, the anniversary of his death.

A Year Gone By...

Gary and I talked at length about what we would do on this day. The four of us chose to spend it with my parents and in-laws. I wanted to do something together that we had not done before. I thought that if we spent the day doing something new, we would be creating new memories and avoiding painful memories. We decided to spend the day in the city of Boston. None of us had been on the famous duck tour. Gary and I thought that this would be something different and somewhat of an adventure.

We planned to take the train into the city very early that Monday morning. Because it was an early train, there was no time to waste. We visited the cemetery once again for the purpose of lighting the perpetual candle. The visit was short. We completed this sad, painful task with heavy hearts. We drove home with the anticipation of the day, hoping it would bring some comfort. We arrived home and my parents arrived immediately after us. We all left for the train. On the surface, everyone seemed to be in good spirits yet, I knew inside all of us were struggling to stay optimistic. We arrived at the train station and waited patiently. The day was sunny and bright. I stood silently while memories swirled in my head. Suddenly my daughter called out to me. A dragonfly had just joined our group. We gathered and stared at this beautiful creature. Aaron was joining us on this difficult day. My extraordinary son had answered my prayer.

We arrived in the big city and the adventure began. There was no time for dawdling. The duck tour was not until the afternoon; therefore, we decided to tour the top of the Prudential building. This proved to be an inspiring event. The view of the city from the top of the building is magnificent. The enjoyment continued from there. We toured the Prudential mall, had a tasty luncheon, and took in the sights of the city life. We even experienced the subway. Of course, the country folk got on the wrong train! Thank goodness for my mother-in-law. She redirected us and even saved us from an additional subway fare. The day ended with the duck tou,r and what a perfect choice we made. If a picture is worth a thousand words, then the souvenir photo tells a happy story. The sparkle in our eyes is just visible to those who knew us. It had not been evident for the past year, yet it seemed to be sneaking out from the pain. It was the right decision to venture to the city on that sad day. We hustled and bustled, leaving no time for thoughts. We shared the day in honor of Aaron.

The ending to this day was especially in honor of Aaron. His favorite meal was Chinese food, especially Crab Rangoon. We arrived back in town at the dinner hour. We chose our favorite Chinese restaurant and headed there to share a meal. The timing was perfect as we arrived at the restaurant at 6:00 pm. We dined and talked about the day. Those of us who favored Crab Rangoon ate lots of it for Aaron. As the fateful hour approached, we were still eating. I looked at my watch and counted the minutes until 7:00 pm. As the clock struck seven, we reached for our glasses and toasted my extraordinary son.

Reflections

I arrived home weary to the bone. Gary lit Aaron's candle. I sat mesmerized by the flame. The past two days had been emotionally draining, and it was finally taking its toll. Sleep was calling out to me. I wanted to close my eyes and escape. I could not sit up any longer, and I went to bed.

As I lay in my bed, I began to reflect on the past year. It seemed impossible to me that three hundred sixty four days had passed since I had seen my son alive. I think back to the moment when the police officer said, "His injuries were too severe; he did not survive the accident." The pain was immediate and similar to a hot knife searing my heart. It took my breath away. Tears flowed freely. The hurt had not lessened. It hurt to the same degree that it had three hundred and sixty-four days ago.

The past year did not soften the pain. The hurt did not go away. To survive, I encased my heart in a box with a door. I've learned control and almost mastered the task of keeping the door shut. At times the door began to open. Anything could trigger it. I might have seen someone who looked like Aaron. Items such as soccer balls, trumpets, dragonflies, red plaid and even black Ford Taurus cars reminded me of

Aaron. I can't explain why sometimes I was able to keep the door closed and other times the door flew open with force. A friend had told me that pain is a testimony to love. If the heart never feels love, then it will never feel pain. I love my son fiercely.

It is that same love that carried me through the pain. I also fiercely love my daughters and my husband. When I was spiraling toward despair, Aaron's words echoed in my mind. He was telling me to be a role model for my two other children. I made myself see their beautiful faces, and I remembered my beautiful girl's accomplishments, and I was able to close the door on pain. Aaron expected me to.

The road I have traveled is not a smooth road. It was bumpy with unexpected pot holes and sudden turns. I believe the road does end. I cannot get to the end without traveling the entire length of it. I try to look ahead to what awaits me. I know there are happy times in my future. New adventures lie ahead. This thought scares me. New adventures may mean a new job or a new home. New people ask questions like, "How many children do you have?" I can easily answer three. However, if they follow my response with, "What are their ages?" I'll have difficulty. Shock appears on their faces when I respond, "My girls are fourteen and eighteen; and my son would be twenty, but he was killed in a car accident one year ago." Strangely enough, I feel their pain when I see the shock in their expression. This frightens me. But I can't hide. I can't stop time. Most of all, I can't change what happened.

I remember Aaron and all of the signs he sends me. I have been inundated with dragonflies, trumpets, soccer balls, red flowers, dreams, scents, feelings, and pictures. I am blessed to have such an extraordinary son. He made me the Mom that I am today and continues to teach me. I choose to believe that heaven exists. I will honor Aaron's request and be the best Mom that I can be to my girls. I will continue to be a loving, supportive wife. I will travel the road that lies ahead of me. I accept the pot holes and the sudden turns. I'll step on the road one foot at a time, anticipating the end. For at the end, Aaron awaits me. I strive for the moment when Aaron stands ahead of me basked in a brilliant, white light. He'll be standing tall and handsome with outstretched arms. I'll walk to him, hold him, and tell him I love him. As I am enveloped in his love, he'll bend and whisper in my ear, "Mom, I am proud of you."

Printed in the United States
60265LVS00003B/151-225

9 781425 953669